D0450320

Relationships in Adolescence

Relationships
in Adolescence

JOHN C. COLEMAN
London Hospital Medical College

ROUTLEDGE & KEGAN PAUL
London and Boston

First published in 1974
by Routledge & Kegan Paul Ltd
Broadway House, 68–74 Carter Lane,
London EC4V 5EL and
9 Park Street,
Boston, Mass. 02108, USA
Set in Monotype Old Style, 11pt, 1pt leaded
and printed in Great Britain by
Western Printing Services Ltd, Bristol
ISBN 0 7100 7868 4
Library of Congress Catalog Card No. 74-81193

To Christopher and Nicholas

Contents

Preface

This book grew out of a determination to undertake research in developmental psychology which would go some way towards bridging the gap between empirical method and practical everyday issues. While there is much to be said for both the pure and the applied points of view where science in general is concerned, developmental psychology has a special responsibility to those most immediately involved with children and adolescents, and it is sad but true that too many psychologists too frequently lose sight of this fact.

The main concern of this work is with the pattern of relationships in adolescence, an area which is directly relevant to all those who have any contact with young people. Two particular assumptions underly the research; first, that adolescence is a major developmental period, and that therefore adequate studies of adolescence must be developmental ones; second, that in such a period of growth and maturation relationships in all areas must inevitably alter, and that much more understanding of this process is needed. Behind the book lies the hope that such findings will provide, for parents no less than for teachers, youth workers and others, an opportunity to get closer to a real understanding of this process, and thereby to the world of adolescence.

Two disclaimers need to be mentioned. In the first instance no attempt has been made to define adolescence, nor to justify the fact that it exists. It has been assumed that it is a period of life which begins at or around puberty, and continues at least until the late teens, though possibly longer. It can be defined in various ways depending on one's perspective, and social, economic or political notions do not always accord with a psycho-logical viewpoint. In the present context it is obviously the psychological definition which has been preferred, and for full discussions of this issue the reader is referred to Muuss (1962) and to Douvan and Adelson (1966). In this study individuals between the ages of eleven and eighteen have been included, a range which has been determined by the secondary school population. However there is no implication that adolescence necessarily stops when a person leaves school, and the extension of the research to an older age range would seem to be essential at a later date.

With regard to the second point, the sample used in the study is a highly selected one where intelligence is concerned. Although the adolescents involved are relatively well distributed with regard to social class, only those of above average intelligence have played a part. This is not a factor which has been stressed continually throughout the book, but it should be noted that all conclusions are based on a limited sample, and cannot be more than preliminary findings which may act as an impetus for others.

Numerous friends and colleagues have contributed to the final product, and to all of them I am deeply grateful. In particular the book would never have been completed without the help of Herbert Phillipson, whose original idea stimulated the project in the first place, Elizabeth Carlile who drew the pictures, Ellen Noonan who struggled with the scoring, Mike Hathorn who spent time on the analysis of the data, Sidney Crown who read and criticized a considerable proportion of the manuscript, and Desmond Pond who created a working environment which made it all possible. In addition, while I am unfortunately unable to mention individuals, I wish to thank all those LEAs, head teachers, and educational psychologists upon whose co-operation and kindness the research was entirely dependent. Finally I must express my gratitude to the adolescents themselves, who so trustingly allowed me to get a glimpse of their hopes and fears, their wishes and anxieties. I hope very much that at least some of them will learn of the result.

I

Theoretical background

Theories of adolescence are badly in need of reorganization. This necessity arises not so much from a paucity of theory, as from the fact that a large proportion of it is scattered and unco-ordinated. In addition, remarkable gaps between theory and experimental evidence are to be found in the literature, and there are times when it seems doubtful whether the theorists do any justice at all to the complexity of adolescent development. In order to provide a background for what follows it will be the aim of this chapter to examine some of the major contributions to the field, and attempt to make some sense of a rather confusing picture. However, because of the enormous variation in both quality and quantity of ideas, and because there is so much convergence in some places, and divergence in others, it is almost impossible to organize the theory by considering individual writers in turn. For this reason a somewhat different approach has been selected, whereby three predominant themes have been identified, around which can be grouped most of the important theoretical formulations. These are (a) the stage theory approach to development, (b) the notion of 'storm and stress', and (c) the issue of 'roles' in adolescence.

Stage theory

The theory of stages is a familiar one in major contributions to the understanding of human development, and two of the best-known theorists—Freud and Piaget—have conceived their ideas within such a framework. Implied in this approach is the notion that development consists of a number of clearly defined stages through which the child has to pass in sequence, i.e. that the attainment of one stage is dependent upon the completion of the previous one. In the theories of both Freud and Piaget the greatest differentiation of stages applies in early childhood, which is explicable in view of the very rapid development that occurs in the first five or six years of life.

In his formulation of psychosexual development Freud suggested that the oral, anal and phallic stages succeed each other comparatively quickly, and are then followed by a relatively longer period of latency, lasting from approximately six or seven until puberty. Once the child reaches puberty he or she enters the genital stage, and Freud made no attempt to differentiate further with regard to the course of adolescent development. One additional important feature of this approach, concerning the notions of fixation and regression, needs to be noted here. Naturally Freud did not envisage that every individual passed smoothly from stage to stage. In his view it is highly probable that individuals, because of anxiety or trauma, will find some stages more difficult than others, and will therefore be less easily able to move on to the succeeding ones. It is this phenomenon which he has called fixation, while regression refers to the individual's return to an earlier stage when under stress or as a defence. While Freud, therefore, laid the foundations for a stage approach to psychosexual development it was left to later writers, such as Blos, to elaborate further upon the process of adolescence.

Piaget's approach to cognitive development followed similar lines. His most closely differentiated stages are in the early years, and the minutely detailed sub-stages of the sensori-motor stage of intellectual development in the first two years contrast markedly with the broader definition of formal operations in adolescence. Again it was left to other writers, in particular Elkind, to fill in the detail of adolescent intellectual development.

Before further consideration is given to the contributions of Blos and Elkind it will be as well to mention here one more example of a broad generalized stage-theory approach—that of Erikson. His approach to human development is based on the view that there is a need for continuous mastery of new tasks, each appropriate for successive age stages. Erikson is thus a writer who espouses a developmental task theory, but also draws upon the ancient notion of the seven stages of man. In his view (Erikson, 1968), life begins with the establishment of *basic trust* in infancy; the maternal relationship is crucial for establishing a foundation upon which to build later trusting relationships. In the second stage the child, by exercising his growing mobility and freedom, begins to establish a sense of *autonomy*, the antithesis of which is seen to be a sense of *shame* and *doubt*. In the third stage the child, if allowed to develop a sufficient sense of responsibility, develops *initiative*, which is contrasted at the opposite end of the pole with feelings of *guilt*. To develop a sense of *industry*, rather than of *inferiority* is the next developmental task, one that is obviously closely linked with the experience of school. Next, in adolescence, comes the issue of *identity*. The young person becomes preoccupied at this time with his view of himself as compared with other people's views of him, and he is faced with the task of adapting his childhood roles and skills to the social and occupational demands of the present. The great danger at this stage, as Erikson sees it, is of *identity diffusion*, stemming from the individual's doubts concerning his sexual, personal and occupational roles. In young adulthood the sixth development task—that of developing *intimacy* rather than *isolation*—is manifestly concerned with the establishment of a close, stable, and mutually satisfying relationship. *Generativity* is the primary task facing the mature adult—the opposite of which is *stagnation*. Finally in old age comes *ego integrity*, the culmination of the life stages, and with it comes fulfilment rather than despair. While this is a broad, almost meta-psychological view of human development, Erikson has in fact elaborated the adolescent stage more than any of the others, and his views will be more closely examined in the next section.

A stage theory approach to
cognitive development
David Elkind, in his paper 'Egocentrism in adolescence' (1967), has been the most notable proponent of an elaborated theory of cognitive development in adolescence. Elkind argues that while egocentrism is not the only parameter of cognitive growth which is of importance, it is the one which is most obviously

common to all stages of maturation, the one which is the most constant thread throughout the developmental process. In order to discuss the nature of egocentrism in adolescence it is therefore necessary to review briefly the other forms of this phenomenon as it is manifested in earlier stages of cognitive development.

Elkind argues that during the *sensori-motor* period the major cognitive task might be regarded as the 'conquest of the object'. Early in life the infant responds to objects according to whether they are present or not in his immediate perception, and so egocentrism at this stage corresponds to a lack of differentiation between the object and the sensory input which it determines. In the next stage, that of *pre-operational thought*, Elkind considers the major task to be the 'conquest of the symbol'. It is at this time that the symbolic function becomes fully active, and this is manifested in the rapid growth of language, the appearance of symbolic play and in early reports of dreams. Here egocentrism is of a different kind; while the child now has the ability to represent mentally an absent object, that is, he has developed object permanence, at this stage he cannot differentiate between symbols and their referents. During this period children believe that the name is implicit in the thing, and that an object cannot have more than one name; for example something can either be a dog or an animal, but not both. In addition if children are asked to explain something to another person, they leave out crucial information. This may be explained both in terms of the child's inability to take the other's point of view, and also by the fact that the child assumes that words carry very much more information than they actually do. Basically the child's egocentrism at this stage lies in his failure to understand the limitations of the symbolic process.

For Elkind the major task of the period of *concrete operations* is that of mastering classes, relations and quantities. The child at this stage gradually comes to grips with notions of conservation, seriation and so on, and the development of these skills enables him to formulate hypotheses and explanations about concrete events. These cognitive operations, however, are seen by the child simply as mental tools, the products of which are on a par with perceptual phenomena. In other words the child at this stage seems unable to differentiate clearly between what is perceptually given and what is mentally constructed. If he formulates a hypothesis it originates with the data, not from within him, and if new data are presented which are contradictory he does not change the hypothesis, but rather prefers to alter the data or to rationalize these in one way or another. Egocentrism at this stage, then, stems from a failure to differentiate adequately between thought processes and perceptual data.

With this background it is now possible to look more closely at adolescent cognitive behaviour—the stage of *formal operations*. For Elkind the major task during this stage can be described as the *conquest of thought*. The use of formal operations, or propositional logic, enables the individual not only to construct 'contrary-to-fact' propositions, but also to think about mental constructions as objects which can be manipulated. It is only at this stage that notions of probability and belief become real and can be utilized effectively. Elkind suggests none the less that it is precisely this new mental maturity which, while freeing the individual from childhood egocentrism, entangles him in a new form of the same thing. The achievement of formal operational thought allows the adolescent to think about not only his own thought, but also the thought of other people. However, it is this capacity to take account of other people's thinking which is the basis of adolescent egocentrism. Essentially he finds it extremely difficult to differentiate between what others are thinking about and his own preoccupations. He assumes, if you like, that if he is obsessed by a thought or a problem then other people must also be obsessed by the same thing. The example given by Elkind is that of the adolescent's appearance. To a large extent teenagers are preoccupied with the way they look to others, and they make the assumption that others must be as involved as they are with the same subject.

Elkind ties this type of egocentrism in with a concept of what he calls 'the imaginary audience'. Because of his egocentrism the adolescent is, either in actual or fantasized social situations, anticipating the reactions of others. However, these reactions are based on the premise that others are as admiring or critical of him as he is of himself. Thus he is continually constructing and reacting to his 'imaginary audience', a fact which, according to Elkind, explains a lot of adolescent behaviour—the self-consciousness, the wish for privacy, the long hours spent in front of a mirror. All these and many other aspects of the teenager's behaviour, it is argued, may be related to the 'imaginary audience'.

There is one other significant aspect of adolescent egocentrism, seen as an example of over-differentiation of feelings, which Elkind calls the 'personal fable'. Possibly because the adolescent believes he is of importance to so many people (his 'imaginary audience') so he comes to see himself and his feelings as very special, even unique. A belief in the unique nature of the individual's misery and suffering is, of course, a familiar theme in literature, and Elkind suggests that it is this belief which underlies the young person's construction of his 'personal fable'. In essence this is the individual's story about himself, the story he tells himself, and it may well include fantasies of omnipotence and immortality. It is not a true story, but it serves a most valuable purpose, and it is particularly well exemplified in some of the most famous adolescent diaries. It is in this sort of material that one can get closest to a belief in the universal significance of the adolescent experience, and it is out of this belief that the 'personal fable' is created.

Elkind argues that these two foundations of adolescent egocentrism—the 'imaginary audience' and the 'personal fable' —are invaluable in understanding adolescent cognitive behaviour, and may be extremely helpful in the treatment of disturbed teenagers. One example he gives is that of adolescent offenders. Here it is often of central importance to help the individual differentiate between the real and the imagined audience, which as Elkind points out often boils down to a discrimination between real and imaginary parents. There is no doubt that these concepts are of considerable importance as theoretical contributions to the understanding of adolescent development, as well as providing illuminating insights into the thought processes of young people. In addition such ideas have obvious links with the next major stage theory to be considered, that of the psychoanalytic writers.

A psychoanalytic stage theory
In his book *On Adolescence*, Blos (1962) makes a distinction

between pre-adolescence, early adolescence, adolescence proper and late adolescence, yet he is clearly not entirely happy with these demarcations. As he writes (pp. 72–3):

In setting up the two phases of early adolescence and adolescence proper, I am in agreement with Helene Deutsch (1944) who divides the adolescence of the girl into 'early puberty' and 'puberty and adolescence'. In the latter phase, which she called 'advanced puberty', heterosexual tendencies are characteristic. I emphasize the characteristic which unifies both, namely object relinquishment and object finding, i.e. the definitive turn towards separation from the family and the gradual hierarchical arrangement of drive components and ego functions. An increasing social self-awareness with attendant anxiety and guilt is an essential ingredient of both these phases.

Naturally any division of phases remains an abstraction; there is no such neat compartmentalization in actual development. The value of this kind of formulation about phases lies in the fact that it focusses our attention on orderly developmental sequences; the phases also make it easier to see the essential psychological modifications and tasks which characterize each phase, as they roughly follow the epigenetic principle of development. Transitions are vague and slow, and beset with oscillating movements; larger or smaller remnants of a seemingly completed phase of adolescent development nevertheless persist for a longer or shorter time during subsequent phases. These irregularities are apt to blur the developmental schedule if it is applied too narrowly and too literally.

In his later work Blos (1967) writes of adolescence more generally as a 'second individuation process'. In this view adolescence is seen as one stage with many themes running through it, some being prominent at one moment, some at another. It is this view, the most coherent and elaborated, which will be considered here.

Blos conceptualizes adolescence, then, as the second individuation process, the first having been completed towards the end of the third year, with the attainment of object constancy. He argues that both periods have a number of features in common. In both there is an increased vulnerability in the

organization of the personality, in both there is an urgent need
for psychological change to meet the major maturational movements, and finally both periods are followed by specific psychopathology should development go awry. What is in infancy a
'hatching from the symbiotic membrance to become an indivi-
duated toddler' (Mahler, 1963) becomes in adolescence the re-
nunciation of dependency on the family and the loosening of
the early infantile ties which have, until puberty, been the
major source of emotional nurturance. It is this notion of disengagement from internalized objects—both loved and hated
figures—which is the keystone of the psychoanalytic view of
adolescence. Disengagement opens the way for the finding of
love and hate objects outside the family. In some senses just the
reverse has happened in early childhood. Here the child, in an
attempt to become separate from the love object, namely the
mother, internalizes her. This allows him to become independent while retaining inside himself a representation of the figure
he needs. In adolescence just the opposite must occur—in order
to gain independence the individual has to give up the internalized infantile object in order to seek new love objects in the
outside world.

Another essential feature of adolescence, as Blos sees it, is
regression. It is a common belief within psychoanalytic theory
that the main threat to the integrity of the personality in early
adolescence is the enormous increase in drive level—the upsurge
of the sexual and aggressive drives which threaten at times to
overwhelm the individual. Blos, however, is convinced that the
danger to the personality stems not only from the strength of
the drives but derives in equal measure from the regressive pull.
He emphasizes that this is the only period in human development during which regression, both of drives and of the ego, is
an obligatory component of normal maturation. Furthermore
this stage-specific regression is seen as being the cause of much
transient maladaptive behaviour, and it accounts for a lot of
the emotional turbulence so characteristic of adolescence. What
is the reason for this regressive pull? Because 'the adolescent
has to come into emotional contact with the passions of his
infancy and early childhood, in order for them to surrender their
original cathexes; only then can the past fade into conscious
and unconscious memories, and only then will the forward

movement of the libido give youth that unique emotional intensity and power of purpose' (1967, p. 178). A phrase from another context—'reculer pour mieux sauter'—describes the process succinctly.

Blos provides a number of examples of what he means by ego regression. One that he chooses is the adolescent's idolization of famous people, especially pop stars and celebrated sportsmen and women. In this phenomenon, he argues, we are reminded of the idealized parent of the younger child. 'Their glorified images constituted an indispensable regulator of the child's narcissistic balance. It should not surprise us that the bedroom walls, plastered with the collective idols, become bare as soon as object libido is engaged in genuine relationships. Then the pictorial flock of transient gods and goddesses is rendered dispensable almost overnight' (1967, p. 174).

Another example of behaviour in which can be recognized reflections of earlier states is the emotional condition similar to 'merger'. Here the individual becomes almost totally absorbed in abstract ideas such as Nature or Beauty, or with political, religious or philosophical ideals. These states, especially those which are drug induced, are sought as a temporary refuge and they act, Blos argues, as safeguards against total merger with the infantile internalized love object.

One further illustration of the effects of the regressive pull may be seen in the adolescent's need for group experiences, or individual relationships and sensations which provide vivid and acute excitement. Blos feels that the frequent and abrupt changes so often seen in these relationships are indications of their essential shallowness, and what appears to be the motive force behind them is not the need for personal contact but the intensity of feeling and agitation of emotion which they provide. He places firmly in this category the need to do things 'just for kicks' which, he argues, is a way of escaping loneliness, boredom and dullness. He also includes here the search for drug and mystical experiences. To describe this condition, Blos uses the term 'affect and object hunger', and he suggests that the adolescent need for intense emotional states may be seen as a means of coping with the inner emptiness which follows the breaking of the infantile ties (Root, 1957). Blos goes on to indicate his belief that both 'object' and 'affect' hunger find some relief in the adolescent's gang or peer group. This social group is often, quite literally, the substitute for the adolescent's family, and within it he may experience all the feelings so essential for individual growth, such as stimulation, empathy, belongingness, the opportunity for role playing, identification, and the sharing of guilt and anxiety.

In the process of disengagement from early objects who are both loved and hated one other throwback to earlier modes of behaviour is very much in evidence, and this is ambivalence. From this stems much of the aggression, the negativism, the indifference and the plainly obstructive behaviour. As seen by Blos, ambivalence accounts for many of the phenomena often considered incomprehensible in adolescent behaviour. The emotional instability of relationships and the contradictions in thought and feeling reflect the fluctuations between loving and hating, active and passive, involvement and non-involvement which underlie object relations in the early years of life, and are reactivated in extreme form once again in adolescence. Nonconformity is an almost universal feature of adolescent behaviour, and Blos believes that, in a sense, it is one of the most adaptive defences against the regressive pull. To illustrate this, he quotes an especially articulate, insightful, adolescent girl (1967, p. 178):

> If you act in opposition to what is expected, you bump
> right and left into regulations and rules. To-day when I
> ignored school—just didn't go—it made me feel very good.
> It gave me a sense of being a person, not just an auto-
> maton. If you continue to rebel and bump into the world
> around you often enough, then an outline of yourself gets
> drawn in your mind. You need that. Maybe, when you
> know who you are, you don't have to be different from
> those who know, or think they know, who you should be.

To summarize, what exactly is the 'individuation' that Blos sees as the major identifying feature of the adolescent stage of development? It appears that for him individuation implies a process whereby the growing person takes increasing responsibility for what he does and what he is, rather than depositing this responsibility on to the shoulders of others, principally of course, his parents. However, it is only through the reanimation of early childhood involvements and patterns of behaviour that the disengagement from infantile attachments can be achieved and that the process of individuation can be successfully worked through. This achievement, then, hinges on regression, which inevitably involves some maladaptive measures. In a paradoxical fashion progress is precluded unless regression is allowed to play its proper part. It appears that the adolescent developmental process entails a continuing tension between forward and backward movement. Each type of movement draws impetus from the other, each defining the other and making it workable. Strangely, much of what must, at first glance, appear to be defensive can in fact more correctly be seen as a precondition for progressive development. Blos suggests that the concept of second individuation makes intelligible the basic paradox of adolescence, because it illuminates the difficult problems of personality structure as well as providing a synthesis for the antagonistic trends of regression and progression.

A number of general issues are posed by a stage theory approach, as Rogers (1972) points out. The one which has the most obvious relevance in the present context is the question of whether adolescence is one stage, a number of sub-stages, or merely a transition from childhood to adulthood. This is an exceptionally difficult question, an answer to which depends on the availability of sufficient empirical evidence to indicate a developmental pattern specific to one age and common to the majority of the population within that age. In addition it is essential to have adequate criteria for the definition of the limits of each stage. In this respect it is interesting to note that more recent thinking (for example Blos) reflects a certain unease with the traditional stage theory approach. It will be suggested in subsequent chapters that stage theory as it is usually understood provides too rigid a framework within which to conceptualize adolescence, and that a more flexible model is required. However this is a large issue, and can be more appropriately considered at a later point in the discussion.

Stability or disruption

'Storm and stress' or 'Sturm und Drang' are instantly recognizable phrases applying to the adolescent period of human development. They carry with them the implication of a time of disruption, of difficulty, of turmoil, even of 'internal civil war' (Rogers, 1972). G. Stanley Hall, an early writer on adolescence, is often credited with being the first to propose this theory. Weiner (1970) quotes Hall as writing thus in 1904 (vol. 2, pp. 74–5):

> The 'teens' are emotionally unstable and pathic. It is the age of natural inebriation without the need of intoxicants, which made Plato define youth as spiritual drunkenness. It is a natural impulse to experience hot and perfervid psychic states, and it is characterized by emotionalism. We see here the instability and fluctuations now so characteristic. The emotions develop by contrast and reaction into the opposite.

Almost all later psychoanalytic writing has supported this view, and Anna Freud's well-known description (1937, pp. 149–50) of adolescence is strikingly similar to that of G. Stanley Hall:

> Adolescents are excessively egoistic, regarding themselves as the centre of the universe and the sole object of interest, and yet at no time in later life are they capable of so much self-sacrifice and devotion. They form the most passionate love relations, only to break them off as abruptly as they began them. On the one hand they throw themselves enthusiastically into the life of the community, and on the other they have an overpowering longing for solitude. They oscillate between blind submission to some self-chosen leader and defiant rebellion against any and every authority. They are selfish and materially minded and at the same time full of lofty idealism. They are ascetic but will suddenly plunge into instinctual indulgence of the most primitive character. At times their behaviour to other people is rough and inconsiderate, yet they themselves are extremely touchy. Their moods veer between light-hearted optimism and the blackest pessimism. Sometimes they will work with indefatigable enthusiasm and at other times they are sluggish and apathetic.

Mention has already been made of the argument, put forward by Blos, that the individuation process during adolescence involves regression, and that such regression does at times lead to what appears to be maladaptive behaviour. However, as

Blos points out, if we look deeper we can see the positive value of this seemingly disturbed behaviour. In fact though, many writers go much further than this. For example Spiegel (1951, 1961) talks of a significant degree of ego dysfunction, and discusses at some length the similarity between adolescence and adult psychotic states. As he says, 'the particular similarity . . . lies in the emergence of primitive defence procedures—belonging to the ego's fear of the strength of instincts' (1961, p. 387).

Ackerman (1958, 1962) is another writer who proposes a thesis which exemplifies the 'storm and stress' point of view; he argues that much of adolescence is characterized by antisocial behaviour, sexual promiscuity, over-conformity with peers, disillusionment, despair and disorientation in relations with family and community. Ackerman's belief is that much of this behaviour is due to the instability of the modern family, which does not provide, according to him, the security necessary for optimal emotional growth.

An additional writer of considerable interest is Phyllis Greenacre. In a fascinating article entitled 'Youth, growth and violence' (1970) she uses psychoanalytic theory to explain 'the nature and course of development in adolescence . . . of symptoms of unrest leading to violence and in the extreme to bomb throwing, as these have appeared during the present revolutionary period' (p. 340). She goes on to say, 'It is necessary further to consider in what ways the present social situation has co-operated or combined with and exaggerated the ordinary problems of adolescence to such an extent as to involve youth fundamentally in the current revolutionary activities' (p. 340). This is an important paper, both because of the subject it tackles and the insight it provides into this pressing social phenomenon. However, the implication in the paper is that violence and unrest are some of the most prominent features of adolescence. In discussing these phenomena, Greenacre makes it clear that in her view such feelings, if not the actual revolutionary behaviour, are common to a large proportion of young people. As she says, adolescence 'is often a time of painful emotional revolution with a great variety of external manifestations as well as of inner stress' (p. 340). It is evident that such a point of view has close links with that of G. Stanley Hall.

Consideration of the 'storm and stress' approach would not be complete without a further look at Erik Erikson's writings. There has already been some mention of his view that the developmental task posed by adolescence is the establishment of identity, the antithesis of which is a lapse into *identity diffusion*. While it is extremely difficult to pin him down, Erikson's general position appears to be that adolescence is a time of identity crisis, that it is a time of very considerable stress in relation to the establishment of a satisfactory identity for the large majority of adolescents. Such a position manifestly implies a period of difficulty and disruption rather than one of stability. However in order to understand Erikson's point of view it is important to mention a further step in his thinking; this involves the notion of adolescence as a *psychosocial moratorium*. Just as, in psychoanalytic theory, the latency stage may be viewed as a time of psychosexual delay, a time when in a sense sexual development is in abeyance, so, argues Erikson, a similar situation applies in adolescence, only with regard to identity. In his view society allows, or even creates, a time of life when the individual may delay major identity decisions, when he may experiment with roles in order that he may discover what sort of a person he is and is not. It could be argued that it is precisely for this reason that there is a crisis at all. The opportunity and even the pressure to experiment freely combined with a vulnerability of personality structure are obvious causal factors which may underlie crises in development. Erikson himself expresses it most clearly when he writes (1968, pp. 163–4):

It is true, of course, that the adolescent, during the final stage of his identity formation, is apt to suffer more deeply than he ever did before or ever will again from a confusion of roles. And it is also true that such confusion renders many an adolescent defenceless against the sudden impact of previously latent malignant disturbances. But it is important to emphasize that the diffused and vulnerable, aloof and uncommitted, yet demanding and opinionated personality of the not too neurotic adolescent contains many necessary elements of a semi-deliberate role experimentation of the 'I dare you' and 'I dare myself' variety. Much of this apparent confusion thus must be considered social play—the true genetic successor of childhood play.

Similarly the adolescent's ego development demands and permits playful, if daring, experimentation in fantasy and introspection.

Thus it becomes apparent that for these writers, for Anna Freud, Blos, Spiegel, Erikson and others, adolescence is a time of life at which very considerable disruption is to be expected. Further, this perspective relates to the large majority of adolescents, rather than being true only of the relative minority who make up the clinical population.

There is, however, a strongly opposing standpoint which has in recent years been supported by many well-known developmental and social psychologists, as well as by prominent psychiatrists. Most recent examples are Douvan and Adelson (1966), Douvan and Gold (1966), Offer (1969), Bealer, Willits and Maida (1969), Offer, Marcus and Offer (1970) and Bandura (1972). Much more will be said concerning this issue in later chapters, and in particular the work of Elizabeth Douvan and her associates has provided a major impetus for the present study. At this point, however, Albert Bandura may be chosen as a good representative of this particular point of view. In an excellent article (1972), which draws heavily upon some experimental evidence published a decade earlier (Bandura and Walters, 1959), it is argued that the 'storm and stress' point of view has been grossly exaggerated. Bandura believes that when one actually looks at the evidence from ordinary middle-class teenagers and their families, it becomes apparent that stability and co-operative, mutually satisfying relationships are much more in evidence than the embattled hostility and disturbance so clearly delineated in the literature. He takes a number of propositions which stem from the 'storm and stress' point of view, and compares them with his research findings. First, it is supposed that during adolescence parents become more controlling and restrictive. However, exactly the opposite picture emerged from the interview data, with both parents and youngsters describing how, as they moved through adolescence, their relationships became easier as they became more able to trust each other. A second supposition concerns independence; it is suggested, as has been noted, that adolescents are involved in a fundamental struggle to emancipate themselves from parental ties. Again Bandura and Walters find no support for this point of view. Bandura writes that in his estimation the establishment of independence from parents has been more or less completed by the time the child becomes adolescent, rather than just beginning at this time. He goes on to say that in his sample the autonomy of the adolescent seemed to pose more of a problem for the parents than for the teenager, many fathers, for example, regretting the companionship they had lost. Finally Bandura considers conformity to peer group values, and here again finds little evidence to support the traditional view. The adolescents whom he interviewed appeared to be discriminating and selective in their choice of reference groups, and there were few signs of 'slavish conformity'. In general, peer group values did not appear to be in direct opposition to family values, nor did it appear that membership of a peer group generated family conflict.

Bandura suggests a number of explanations for the discrepancies between theory and experimental evidence. Amongst others he mentions mass media sensationalism, generalization from inappropriate samples, such as cross-cultural data or evidence from deviant groups of adolescents, the rigidity of the stage theory approach which glosses over individual variation, and finally the self-fulfilling prophecy—if society labels adolescents as wild and rebellious, then wild and rebellious they will become. On the other hand, it may well be that Bandura and others with similar views who have based their findings on interview data have fallen victim to a simplistic fallacy. Can one be sure that what teenagers tell strangers about their conflicts and anxieties is to be accepted at face value? It may well be that the conflicts and turmoil that the psychoanalysts talk of are not surface, wholly conscious phenomena, and possibly different, more sophisticated experimental methods may be necessary to allow adolescents and parents to express some of the more fundamental elements in their relationships. In any event this is an issue to which further attention will need to be directed.

One other important body of opinion which is in opposition to the psychoanalytic 'storm and stress' approach is to be found in the social psychological literature. Bengtson (1970), in his discussion of the 'generation gap', indicates a number of writers who provide support for Bandura's position, and perti-

nent examples may be found in the field of attitudes. One prediction, derived from the 'storm and stress' point of view, might
be that a considerable discrepancy in attitudes between adults
and adolescents will exist, especially in relation to emotive
issues such as sexual behaviour. However, studies by Bell (1966)
and Reiss (1968) suggest that while there was a considerable
generational change in sexual attitudes, especially with regard
to pre-marital sex, before and after 1900, no such change seems
to have occurred between the generations of the present-day
teenager and his parents. A further supporting study by Walsh
(1970), involving a survey of the patterns of pre-marital sexual
behaviour of college students, showed that these were remarkably similar to the patterns which characterized their parents'
generation.

Parallel findings are available where political attitudes are
concerned. For example Thomas (1971), in a study of sixty
politically active parents (thirty liberal and thirty conservative)
and their teenage children, found that 'children of highly politi-
cized parents tend to be like their parents both in their political
attitudes and their political behaviour'. Westby and Braungart
(1968) came to much the same conclusion. They found considerable similarity between student members of an American revolutionary group (Young Americans for Freedom) and their
parents with respect to political identification, and they argue
that a stratification theory explains political activism much
better than a generational theory. The latter would presuppose
that the young wish to rebel against their parents and therefore
demonstrate against symbolic authority figures, yet the evidence
suggests that these attitudes cut across generational lines. In
addition to this, a number of studies have looked at the continuity or discontinuity of behaviour and values through a
number of generations. The work of Aldous and Hill (1965) and
Hill and Aldous (1969) is particularly relevant here. They show
that over three generations, while behaviour concerning practical issues (e.g. division of household tasks) has changed,
fundamental value systems such as religious beliefs have hardly
altered at all. Furthermore it is of particular interest to see that
in their studies they found greater overall similarity between
middle-aged parents and their children, than between the
parents and the grandparents.

Thus it can be seen that there is considerable weight of evidence, primarily based on empirical studies, which contributes to a view of adolescence as being very much more stable and conforming than would appear from the mass media, the man in the street or the psychoanalytic writers. The controversy is one of the fundamental issues to which this book is directed, and so it will provide a continuous theme throughout the succeeding chapters. Before it is dropped for the moment, however, it might be as well to consider briefly some possible explanations for the fundamental differences between the two approaches. The obvious problem of methodology has already been mentioned—no-one should expect the interview technique to elicit the same material as would be expressed, for example, on a projective test. Closely allied to this problem is the question of levels of personality (Coleman, 1969a). The level of verbal report, or of 'public communication', is not necessarily congruent with the private or symbolic level, especially in situations where a considerable amount of anxiety is present. The third possibility, which is also of considerable importance, is the difference in populations upon which theories are based. It would be surprising if the psychoanalysts, who have made such an overwhelming contribution to the theoretical literature, were not influenced by the context in which they meet adolescents. Inevitably their frame of reference must be affected by the clinical nature of their contact—a very different contact from that which Bandura's interviewers would have had with ordinary middle-class teenagers in the context of their own home or school. All these are points which will require elaboration, but they are important to have in mind before consideration is given to the empirical evidence presented in the following chapters.

Role theory

Many writers who have attempted to make sense of adolescence have done so by using sociological concepts, and the consequent analysis has frequently been in terms of role or self theory. It is argued (Elder, 1968) that at least two-thirds of a person's life is characterized by role engagements, and by the building of a role repertoire which constitutes a crucial facet of the self. The years between childhood and adulthood, as a period of 'emerging identity', are seen as particularly relevant to the construction of this role repertoire, for the following reasons. Features of adolescence such as growing independence from authority figures, involvement with peer groups, and unusual sensitivity to the evaluations of others all provoke role transitions and discontinuity, varying in their intensity, of course, as a function of both social and cultural context. Furthermore, any inner change or uncertainty has the effect of increasing the individual's dependence on others, and this applies particularly to the need for reassurance and support for one's view of oneself. The effects of major environmental changes are also relevant in this context. Different schools, the move from school to university or college, leaving home, taking a job, all demand involvement in a new set of relationships, which in turn lead to different and often greater expectations and a substantial reassessment of self and identity.

The view that major role transitions lead to personality change, and that adolescence is such a period of transition, is one which has been supported by numerous writers. Prominent examples are Mannheim (1943), Sarbin (1964) and Sullivan (1950, 1953). The last-named, stating his theory of the continuity and discontinuity of the self, writes (quoted in Thompson, 1964):

Alteration of the self . . . occurs when the significant people in our lives change and in adapting to the new situation certain characteristics may be pushed aside and others allowed to emerge. This change can be either in a constructive or destructive direction.

In discussing adolescence as a transitional period of personality development Elder (1968) takes the theory a step further by distinguishing two types of role change or role discontinuity. On the one hand the adolescent experiences *intra-role change*. In this the individual is exposed to new role demands, since as he gets older expectations gradually increase. His role remains the same, but within that role different things are expected of him—his teacher may expect better performance, his parents more independence, and so on. On the other hand, the individual also acquires entirely *new roles*. Evidently this discontinuity is more abrupt, and is often more difficult to cope with. The change, for example from school to full-time work, often requires very considerable adaptation, and remnants of the dependent student role are often seen in the young worker. The acquisition of new roles is usually coupled with gradual changes of an intra-role nature, and the two facilitate or hinder each other depending on factors such as the part played by the parents or other significant figures, the relevance of past learning and skills to new role demands, the range of the adolescent's role repertoire, and so on. In general it is argued that adolescents experience more or less discontinuity, and that as the degree of role discontinuity increases, successful adaptation to the new set of role demands becomes more problematic.

Self-image is another concept which is often seen as being closely related to role development, and a number of writers have contributed significantly to theory by considering this aspect of adolescent personality. For example Rosenberg (1965, p. 3) writes:

> At this stage of development—between about fifteen and eighteen years of age—the individual tends to be keenly concerned with his self-image. What am I like? How good am I? What should, or might I, become? On what basis shall I judge myself? Many adolescents are consumed with questions of this sort.

Rosenberg suggests three reasons for this phenomenon of heightened self-awareness and concern with self-image. First, adolescence is a time of such major change, both physical and psychological, that faced with pressures of this kind any individual will be forced to re-assess and take stock of himself. Second, adolescence, particularly late adolescence, is an age at which many fundamental decisions present themselves. It is at this time that the initial occupational decision is usually taken, and also critical sexual choices are often made between the years of seventeen and twenty. As Rosenberg says, when a major factor in these decisions is the individual's view of what sort of a person he is, it is not surprising that the self-image comes into the foreground. Finally, adolescence is marked by particular status ambiguity. Society has no clearly defined expectations of the individual during his adolescent years, and therefore responds to him in a manner which must appear ambiguous—at times demanding childlike obedience and at others expecting the self-confidence and independence of an adult. Rosenberg argues that it is just this sort of ambivalence in others which brings into question the adolescent's own self-image.

A representative study based on role theory may help to fill out the picture. Orville Brim (1965), in a paper entitled 'Adolescent personality as self-other systems', not only describes an intriguing and inventive piece of research, but also argues cogently the sociologist's view of personality development (p. 156):

> Personality can be viewed as a set of learned self-other relationships or systems, each of these built up from thousands of remembered expectations of others, from the appraisal of one's behaviour both by these others and by himself, from the perceived success or failure of the action, and from the rewards and punishments by society through its agents—parents, teachers, peers, etc. It follows that we should attempt to describe personality by reference to the individual's perceptions of himself and his behaviour, and of the social organisation in which he lives. We should be interested in the kinds of people he says are of the greatest significance to him, and interested in what he thinks others expect him to do, and in what they think about his performances. We should also know whether or not he accepts what others prescribe for him as right and legitimate, or whether he thinks their expectations are unfair; we should know about his relationships, as he sees them, to these significant others, whether he likes them, trusts them, thinks they are consistent in their behaviour, whether the relationship is of long or short duration, and so on. . . .

In his research Brim examined a number of aspects of role structure, but focused particularly on the prescriptions or expectations that other people hold with regard to the adolescent's behaviour. Each teenager in the sample was asked for his perception of the role prescriptions held for him by his father, mother, friends and teacher. These expectations were elicited with reference to the three main social contexts or role areas in the adolescent's life, i.e. family, peer group and school. The research was conducted using descriptions of how one might wish to behave (e.g. 'get along well with brothers and sisters', 'be popular with girls', 'act less smart than I really am') and asking adolescents how significant persons such as parents or teachers felt about these prescriptions. In this research Brim was asking in what way these various role prescriptions fitted together. Were they organized in terms of specific roles so that the adolescent would think of himself as a friend at one time, a student at another, and a son or daughter at still another? On the other hand, is the organization in terms of more general themes, irrespective of role, so that some adolescents will be oriented towards achievement, some towards friends and social acceptance, some perhaps towards family cohesion? The findings showed that role prescriptions fitted together and could be analysed into a number of different factors. Some of these factors, such as 'being serious and able to take responsibility' appeared to emanate from one significant figure (in this case the father) and concerned one role (here the son or daughter role). On the other hand some of the factors (for example 'academic achievement') are prescribed by many different people and therefore cut across individual roles and relationships.

Brim argues that such information concerning the ways in which role prescriptions are organized in the adolescent personality is of enormous importance because it leads directly to an understanding of the significant sources of motivation, and therefore of personality development. Brim's view is that motivation is generated by interpersonal relationships. During childhood the individual develops a learned desire to conform to other people's expectations and to their role prescriptions, and his sense of security and acceptance depends on his perceptions of his conformity. How good or bad he feels will depend on the degree to which he lives up to the expectations of other people. Naturally the importance of this particular type of self-appraisal to the adolescent varies according to the significance of the other person to him, and it is well known that the adolescent has a wide range of reference figures, who will not necessarily be the immediate teacher, parent or friend. None the less the fact remains that, from the sociologist's point of view, a combined knowledge of salient figures and role prescriptions will provide the critical information necessary to make sense of the adolescent's motivation and self-esteem.

This particular approach contributes not only to a theory of adolescence, but also, as Brim points out, it can provide helpful leads in the task of portraying individual personalities. What he has in mind here is the degree to which the adolescent is characterized by specific clusters of role prescriptions. For example some adolescents will score on factors associated with specific roles, some on factors related to individual themes, while some will be characterized by a diversity of factors or by factors which cut across roles, themes and relationships. Obviously every youngster will manifest a different profile of scores, but the factors which Brim derived from his study can quite clearly be used as reference points in the difficult task of describing personality.

The contribution of role or self theory is an important one because it contrasts sharply with the previously mentioned approaches. It is particularly helpful in that it stresses the social context of the maturing individual, and perceives the sources of motivation as lying as much outside the individual as within. However, as an approach it is limited by the absence of specific developmental assumptions, and the model which follows from it must be a predominantly static one. Both the other two approaches similarly imply models of development, each with obvious strengths and weaknesses. Mention has already been made of the rigidity of stage theory, and the controversy surrounding the 'storm and stress' approach has also been given some airing. It will be the task of the present study to re-examine and to compare these approaches in the light of the empirical evidence which forms the body of this work.

2

The problem and the method

In the preceding chapter three major themes have been examined, and it has proved possible to group together around each of these themes a set of theoretical contributions which go some way to making a relatively coherent picture. The three themes are not necessarily related, but each adds a different and important perspective to the notion of the adolescent individual. In view of this it may seem strange that the chapter began by referring to a general state of disarray in adolescent psychology, and now that some of the theoretical ground has been covered, this statement requires elaboration.

First, many of the theoretical contributions, the large majority in fact, are concerned with limited areas of development. They are piecemeal statements or propositions which make no attempt to tie up with other aspects of development or with the broader picture of the adolescent process. Two particularly good examples which are distinguished because of their importance are Erikson's theory of identity and Elkind's ideas concerning egocentrism in cognitive development.

Second, it will already have become clear that there is a very considerable degree of controversy in this area of developmental psychology, and there are a number of issues, such as conflict or disruption during adolescence, where the empirical evidence is in direct contradiction to the theory. Douvan and Adelson (1966, p. 8) describe in vivid terms how they perceive the situation:

> The empirical literature most of the time is directionless
> following a current fancy or simply following its own
> nose. . . . The other literature, the literature of large

ideas—does not find the empirical writing to be relevant to its concerns, and so it in turn remains stagnant and insular.

The third area of concern is that there are obvious topics of importance which have not received the attention they deserve from the theorists. These are topics which are clearly a part of the overall picture, and yet they attract too little speculation, and even less empirical investigation. The role of friendship, the psychological aspects of sexual development, the place of solitude and, perhaps most important, attitudes to authority are all striking examples of salient issues urgently in need of clarification.

Finally one of the major contentions of this book is that the available theory does not do justice to the phenomenon. Adolescence cannot adequately be comprehended simply as one stage of development. It is a period of life which extends over at least six or seven crucial years, and thus it involves a developmental process. The child is not static, he changes at an enormous rate, and any image of an eleven- and an eighteen-year-old side by side illustrates the unrealistic nature of the concept of a single stage. Theories of adolescence must acknowledge this fact. To be comprehensive they must involve some notion of change and transition; adolescence, if it is to be set realistically within a descriptive and explanatory framework, must be viewed as a process rather than as a category.

In studying relationships in adolescence and in attempting to move towards a more unified and acceptable theory there appear to be a number of points to remember. First, research should not concentrate only on the superficial or surface aspects of the problem, such as those which might be elicited by interview techniques, but should try to explore deeper levels of relationships and attempt to obtain some picture of the more private world of the normal adolescent. Second, studies should provide empirical data from which theoretical propositions can be derived, for it seems particularly important for any further findings to bridge rather than widen the gap between theory and research already referred to above.

Third, both research design and whatever theory follows from it must acknowledge the developmental nature of adolescence. It is of little value to conceptualize adolescents as all belonging to one category or sub-culture, distinguished by the single fact that they are passing through a particular stage of life. On the other hand it is hardly more helpful to solve the problem by postulating sub-stages such as 'early', 'middle' and 'late' adolescence. Adolescence is a dynamic process, and the comprehensive theory will be the one that, rather than implying a static quality, recognizes change as an essential feature of this period.

Finally research methodology must be holistic in its orientation. Relationships interact, and there will be little point, for example, in examining the young person's heterosexual relationships without at the same time looking at his relationships with his friends, his parents and with other significant figures in his world. Although it may be necessary to break down the total pattern into manageable units for study and analysis, the system is a large, interlocking, interrelated one, and any conclusions must recognize this fact.

Method

Subjects

This study is a cross-sectional one, and has involved boys and girls at four ages during the adolescent period. Chronological age has been used as the independent variable, though this does have obvious weaknesses which will be further discussed below. The four age groups consist of eleven-, thirteen-, fifteen- and seventeen-year-olds, and an attempt has been made to include approximately a hundred boys and a hundred girls at each of the four ages, making a total of eight hundred. Details of the actual sample composition will be found in Appendix A, table A.

There are in the literature numerous discussions concerning the relative merits of cross-sectional and longitudinal studies (e.g. Mussen, 1960), and it is unnecessary to review these in any great detail here. However it is essential to clarify the limitations that the use of a cross-sectional design imposes. Tanner's (1962) discussion of this problem is a useful starting point. In this he points out that cross-sectional data provide a poor indication of rate or velocity of growth, and no indication at all of the variability of rate or velocity. To be more specific, if one was interested in the rate at which height increased during adolescence, then it would be preferable to derive these data from a longitudinal study, but if one was concerned with the variability of height increase, then it would be essential to do so. However, cross-sectional data do provide what might be called distance curves of growth, or to put it another way, they indicate the mean age of a group reaching a particular maturational stage. Thus, for example, a cross-sectional study could indicate what proportion of a group at any one time has reached a particular stage, or what proportion possess a particular characteristic. These are in fact exactly the questions to be asked in the present study. The concern here will be primarily with the presence or absence of certain phenomena (i.e. types of relationships) at different ages, and considerable caution will be exercised in considering growth rates. In addition, it should be clear at the outset that there will be no indication of the duration of a particular type of relationship; for example while it will be possible to determine how many fifteen-year-old girls are uneasy in heterosexual situations, it will not be possible to indicate how many of these were uneasy at thirteen and likely still to be uneasy at seventeen. That type of information can only be derived from a longitudinal study.

Tanner also argues cogently against the use of chronological age as a variable in adolescent growth studies. He points out that because of the variation in intensity and duration of the adolescent growth spurt the use of chronological age is in most circumstances far too vague. For example to say that a child is twelve years old provides only minimal information concerning his physiological maturation, and tells nothing of whether he has reached puberty, is well past it, or still has another eighteen months to go. Tanner suggests four possible measures of physiological age, which is, in his view, a more reliable criterion of the stage of development reached by the individual; these are skeletal age, dental age, morphological age and age derived from secondary sex characteristics. Tanner himself, however, acknowledges the major difficulties involved in measuring and actually using any of these with a large sample, and in any event in the present study the practical problems would have been insurmountable.

This having been said, it is important to recognize that the use of chronological age, apart from its practical advantages, has been preferred for another, more important reason in the present instance. The fact is that chronological age defines, in the large majority of cases, the class in which the child is placed in school, and is therefore the major factor in determining the social group to which he belongs. Two eleven-year-olds may differ greatly in their degree of physiological maturation, but will be members of the same classroom and therefore share to a very considerable extent mores, values and experiences. Because of this the problem becomes one of choosing between a social and a physiological definition of age, and in this study the former has been preferred.

Finally it is important here to say something about the adolescents who participated in the study—who were they, where did they come from, and how were the schools chosen? As a result of experience in previous studies (Coleman, 1969b, 1970) it was decided to restrict the sample to boys and girls who were of at least above average intelligence, primarily because of the tests used, and the intellectual demands involved in being able to respond fully to these. This meant that it was only possible to draw from grammar schools, top streams in comprehensive schools and academically successful day public schools. Since the total group was to be a large one, it was feasible to attempt to select schools so that the sample would, with respect to social class, be approximately representative of the total population in the country. While this was not entirely possible, a fairly close match was achieved in view of the difficulties involved in sampling from school populations (see Appendix A, table C). The criterion for social class in this context was father's occupation, which information it was possible to elicit from the children since their participation in the study was anonymous. In the event the schools involved were two public schools in the Greater London area, and state schools in an inner London Borough and in one of the Home Counties. In each school whole classes were used, and all children in the selected classes were included in the study.

Procedure

In the present research design a projective approach has been used. It has already been mentioned that many of the important studies of adolescence have been based on interview techniques, and some of the difficulties implicit in this method have been discussed. Clearly the interview has many advantages: it is flexible, it is direct, it is infinitely variable to suit the needs of the experimenter, and it can be open-ended so that the inter- viewer can make further enquiries if further information is needed. In spite of all this it is obviously important to ask whether the interview is the most appropriate means of obtain- ing information from the adolescent, particularly if that infor- mation is of a personal nature. On the one hand the individual is more sensitive during adolescence than at any other time in his life about his personal feelings and anxieties, especially when faced with a strange interviewer, and on the other hand it seems probable that he will be largely unaware of the major forces which motivate and determine his interpersonal be- haviour. For these two reasons there seems to be a strong case for developing and using other techniques which will not be so directly threatening, and might at the same time tap some of the attitudes and feelings of which the individual is unaware.

One obvious example of this approach is the work of Powell (1955), whose ingenious use of a word-association technique enabled him to elicit indirectly the degree of conflict associated with various types of relationship by using reaction times as source data. Another type of source datum is imaginative material, expressed in response to stimuli similar to those used in projective tests. Such stimuli may be inkblots, they may be unstructured pictures of people in various situations, or sentence- stems as used, for example, by Musgrove (1964). In previous studies (Coleman, 1967, 1968, 1969b, 1969c, 1970) the author has experimented with all these types of stimuli in attempts to assess the feasibility and the validity of such a method for the study of adolescent development. It is, of course, in no way a novel or revolutionary approach, and it has certainly received considerable attention in the past (Henry, 1960; Bronfenbrenner and Ricciuti, 1960). As a method it is based on the view that by completing or structuring ambiguous material the individual projects something of himself into his responses. Frank (1939, pp. 402–3) expresses it well when he writes:

we may approach the personality and induce the individual
to reveal his way of organizing experience by giving him a
field (objects, materials, experiences) with relatively little

structure and cultural patterning so that the personality can project upon that plastic field his way of seeing life, his meanings, significances, patterns, and especially his feelings. Thus we elicit a projection of the individual personality's *private world* because he has to organize the field, interpret the material, and react affectively to it.

Further characteristics of the approach are that the stimuli are less directly relevant to the individual than, say, the questions in an interview, thus enabling him to remain less aware of the personal significance of his responses (Coleman, 1969a). In addition, unlike many empirical instruments, there are no right or wrong answers, allowing thereby an almost infinite range of possible solutions.

These characteristics have not unnaturally given rise to considerable criticism of the projective method on the part of experimental psychologists, but it is important to remember that on the whole the criticisms have been directed towards the use of projective tests in the assessment of an individual, rather than towards their use in the study of groups (Buros, 1965; Goldberg and Werts, 1966; Wyatt, 1967). In a group situation the projective stimulus can be used in exactly the same way as any standard perceptual stimulus (such as a word, a line, a geometrical shape or a visual illusion), and as long as it is possible to construct a reliable scoring procedure which takes account of the nature of the responses, the use of projective stimuli is no different methodologically from the use of any other standard stimulus.

It is exactly this approach which has been taken in the present study. While there are many difficulties involved in the use of imaginative material as source data, none the less, the problems outlined at the beginning of this chapter which are implicit in studying relationships in adolescence have to be met, and they are likely to be met more effectively by the projective approach than by any other. Such an approach provides both quantitative and qualitative data, it allows individuals freedom to vary, it is less threatening than any other technique of this sort and so is more likely to get closer to the private world, and it has the great advantage that it can be administered in a group setting.

Two tests were used, both of them modifications of well-known projective techniques. The tests were designed to complement each other exactly, with items in one test having equivalents in the other. Since relationships were being studied it was decided that each test should have items which concerned specific types of relationship, and in effect items covered one-person, two-person, three-person and group situations. The construction of the tests was very much influenced by the object-relations theory of personality which is associated with the Tavistock Clinic (Fairbairn, 1952), and particularly by Herbert Phillipson's extension of these ideas. The two tests used were a sentence completion test, and a picture-thematic test which was an amalgam of the Object Relations Technique (Phillipson, 1955), the Thematic Apperception Test (Murray, 1943) and some specially designed cards. Both tests will be found in Appendix B.

The tests were printed, so that a copy of each could be given to all children in the classroom simultaneously. They were presented as tests of imagination, and all subjects were told that the experimenter was interested in the way people changed as they grew older, and that identical tests were being given to large numbers of other boys and girls of different ages. The tests were completed, usually in two separate sessions, and everyone was provided with a full explanation of the study at the end.

Naturally the study provided an overwhelming mass of data, which in essence consisted of the responses of boys and girls at four ages to a series of interpersonal situations, ranging from solitude to heterosexual relationships, friendship, parental relationships, and the large group. These responses were in the form of both stories and sentence completions, and such individual data inevitably created major difficulties for scoring and analysis. It was decided to analyse these data initially in the simplest manner possible, and so all responses, both stories and sentences, were scored as falling within one of four categories: *Constructive* (where the situation or relationship is seen as being in some way helpful, valuable, supportive or enjoyable), *Negative* (where the situation or relationship is described as destructive, unhelpful, irritating or to be avoided), *Neutral* (where no evaluative statement is made), and *Ambivalent* (where both a Constructive and Negative view is taken within the same response). This breakdown forms the major analysis of the study,

although in almost all areas further analyses have been undertaken with respect to particular issues or questions. Details of
these will be found in the relevant chapters, and statistical data
and further information concerning the scoring procedure may
be found in Appendix C.

Finally it should be noted that *chi square* has been used to
determine the significance of the differences between age groups
and between the two sexes where the expression of Constructive,
Negative and Neutral themes are concerned. However, in all
other cases statistical analyses have not been carried out, and
the figures have been left to speak for themselves. The reason
for this is that in some cases very small numbers have been
involved, and it seemed confusing to carry out tests in some
situations and not in others. Thus all data relating to the major
categories of response have been subjected to statistical analysis,
but this has not been applied to further explorations of the
evidence.

3

Solitude and self-image

It is no coincidence that in considering the empirical evidence concerning the development of relationships in adolescence the issues of solitude and self-image are to be dealt with first, for both of these may be viewed as foundations upon which the young person's interactions with others are based. On the one hand a relationship is in part defined by its antithesis, which is in effect separation, and it is undoubtedly true that much more sense can be made of the way an individual feels and acts when he is with others if something is known of the way he feels about being on his own. On the other hand, as writers such as Rosenberg indicate so clearly, behaviour in a relationship is affected not only by the responses of the other but also by the way in which the individual perceives himself, which is why the issue of self-image plays such a prominent part in the sociologist's view of adolescent development.

There is one further point. In this study an attempt is being made to look at developmental aspects of relationships, and one possibility which needs continually to be borne in mind is that the patterns which are being investigated will be closely linked. Relationships with parents will very probably be connected to and affected by relationships with friends or with other authority figures, and the same may well be true of attitudes to solitude and changes in self-image. The degree to which relationships of different sorts run parallel, and their interaction with feelings of identity, are extremely important issues, and it is hoped that the empirical evidence to be considered will go at least some way towards their clarification.

Solitude

It is an interesting fact that in developmental psychology solitude is not a topic which has received anything more than passing attention, and therefore it will be as well to consider briefly the ways in which it may be relevant to adolescence. Mention has already been made of Piaget's notion of 'object constancy'—the ability to accept that an object exists even when it cannot be directly perceived. It is upon this cognitive skill that the child bases the gradually developing ability to internalize the mother figure, to accept that she exists even if not physically present, and thus to develop a gradually increasing tolerance of solitude. Furthermore it is for this reason that between the ages of one and three the child is so vulnerable to separation experiences (Yarrow, 1964; Bowlby, 1969; Schaffer, 1971); the awareness of the mother exists, the internalization is not yet complete. In assessing a three- or four-year-old consideration is often given to whether the child has the ability to play on his own for short periods, or whether he is continually clinging and demanding adult attention. Undoubtedly some partly subjective standard of maturity is applied in the expectation of what children of different ages should be able to tolerate. Much the same holds with regard to the assessment of adolescent behaviour. It is of interest to know how much time the individual spends on his own—again a certain amount is expected, but too much or too little might be considered worrying.

In so far as the development of this ability has been conceptualized at all, it has been assumed that tolerance of solitude increases with age, though whether this is a linear development through childhood and adolescence is apparently unknown. In descriptions of adolescent behaviour it is not uncommon to find such terms as 'moody' or 'withdrawn', and it is often assumed that most young people at some time pass through a stage when they like to be left on their own.

In view of the limited information available it is not possible to make firm predictions concerning the adolescent's feelings about solitude. However in a previous study, using a small sample of working-class adolescent girls, the author (Coleman, 1970) found that fear of solitude decreased significantly with age. It may well be, therefore, that this pattern holds for a wider range of young people. In the present study the following questions need to be asked. 'At what age is fear of solitude greatest?' 'Is there a stage at which adolescents show a particular wish for solitude?' and 'Will there be a difference between boys and girls in this respect?'

The evidence
The evidence is drawn from the responses to two items on the sentence completion test (see Appendix B). These are sentence no. 5 (WHEN THERE IS NO ONE ELSE AROUND I . . .) and no. 12 (IF A PERSON IS ALONE . . .), and the results are illustrated in figure 3.1. It will be recalled from the previous chapter that a Constructive score implies the constructive use of or positive attitude to solitude (e.g. 'WHEN THERE IS NO ONE ELSE AROUND I am happy because I can do what I like'), while a Negative score has been assigned where solitude is perceived as frightening, upsetting or in some way detrimental to the individual (e.g. 'IF A PERSON IS ALONE they are scared').

The graphs are based on sentence 12 alone, but reference to Appendix C will show an identical trend in the results derived from sentence 5. The most striking features of these graphs are the relatively steady increase in Constructive scores as a function of age, the concomitant decrease in Negative scores, and the fact that, although the direction of the trends is similar for boys and girls, the latter express a higher proportion of Constructive themes and a lower proportion of Negative themes. In looking at these data it is possible already to answer some of the questions posed earlier, for it is clear that the ability to enjoy or make use of solitude comes with age, and there is certainly no evidence to show that in early adolescence there is a particular wish for solitude. On the contrary it is among the younger groups that specific fears and anxieties about being on one's own are expressed, as the following responses to the sentence-completion test illustrate:

Eleven-year-old boy: 'IF A PERSON IS ALONE he gets nervous.'
Eleven-year-old boy: 'IF A PERSON IS ALONE they might steal something.'
Twelve-year-old boy: 'IF A PERSON IS ALONE you often see him or her do very strange things.'

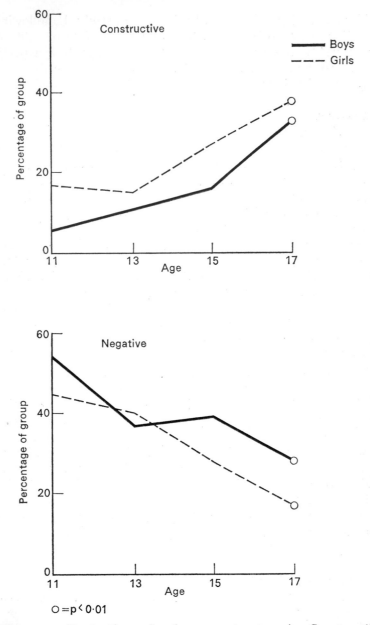

Figure 3.1 *Proportions of each age group expressing Constructive and Negative themes on sentence 12*

Eleven-year-old boy: 'WHEN THERE IS NO ONE ELSE AROUND I do things that look as though I've gone mad.'
Eleven-year-old girl: 'WHEN THERE IS NO ONE ELSE AROUND I feel that a man is going to attack me.'
Eleven-year-old girl: 'WHEN THERE IS NO ONE ELSE AROUND you are lonely as if the world was empty.'
Twelve-year-old girl: 'IF A PERSON IS ALONE they feel sad not wanted.'
Eleven-year-old girl: 'IF A PERSON IS ALONE she feels frightened more than if she was with others.'

It would, of course, be misleading to imply that the younger adolescents' only feelings about solitude are negative. There are certainly individuals of this age who express constructive themes, for example:

Eleven-year-old girl: 'WHEN THERE IS NO ONE ELSE AROUND I often wish it was always so private and peaceful.'

In addition, note may be taken of a delightful but rather pathetic story written by a thirteen-year-old girl in response to picture 10 of the picture story test (see Appendix B):
This is a picture of a groom looking out of a window into the bright sun. His quarters are above the stables in the loft. The room is dark and sweet smelling. His bed is in the hay. He gets up every morning and opens the window to the sun. He looks out across the country and wonders when he will escape this life for an even better one, and he thinks. He finds it is a good life because he is free with no responsibilities, and he is with horses which he knows and loves not with unreliable human beings.

None the less, it is generally true to say that the large majority of constructive themes are expressed by the older groups, of which the following are examples:

Fifteen-year-old girl: 'IF A PERSON IS ALONE they can see things in a new perspective.'
Eighteen-year-old girl: 'IF A PERSON IS ALONE they have time to think about life.'

Seventeen-year-old boy: 'IF A PERSON IS ALONE he can probably do things a lot better than if people are present.'
Seventeen-year-old boy: 'IF A PERSON IS ALONE he chooses his own path.'

Perhaps, though, the last word may be left to a fifteen-year-old girl who wrote: 'IF A PERSON IS ALONE it can be very stimulating and vital or horribly cold and sad.'

There are two immediate questions which are raised by the consideration of these findings. On the one hand some explanation is necessary for the high level of anxiety among the younger age group, and on the other an elucidation of the differences between boys and girls is required. As far as the first is concerned, it seems probable that this result has something to do with the increase in impulse life around puberty, and the corresponding fears of loss of self-control which must come with this. Much has been made in the psychoanalytic literature of the pressure upon the ego at this time. Fears of being alone, and the wish to be with others, especially if these are people who can be trusted, would link up well with such a point of view, particularly if attention is paid to the actual themes expressed by the eleven- and twelve-year-olds. The fear that one might steal, do strange things, or even look mad to others must be an extremely potent factor in wanting to avoid being alone.

With respect to the sex differences, these are in a sense exactly the opposite of what might have been expected in view of the evidence suggesting higher levels of dependency among girls (Kagan and Moss, 1962; Douvan and Adelson, 1966). One explanation may be simply that boys have greater difficulties in impulse control generally; alternatively degrees of maturity may provide the answer. Since girls are more advanced in some areas, this may apply also to the ability to tolerate solitude. For the moment, however, these issues can be put to one side until further evidence has been considered.

Self-image

Reference has already been made to Erik Erikson's concept of adolescence, and it will be recalled that at the heart of his approach is a concern with identity, a concern with the way in which the adolescent sees himself. While in his own writings Erikson has not paid much attention to empirical studies of self-image, nevertheless the impact of his formulation has been extremely widespread. The developmental task of adolescence is seen as one of securing identity and avoiding identity diffusion. This concept has had considerable effect upon the way in which adolescence has come to be perceived, and certain very important undertones have come to be associated with it. When Erikson uses phrases such as 'identity crisis' (1963) and 'the psychopathology of everyday adolescence' (1969) the implication in his thinking is clear. He is arguing that some form of disturbance is to be expected in the normal adolescent, especially with regard to his view of himself. Furthermore Erikson believes that this crisis is most likely to occur towards the end of the adolescent period.

In evaluating such an approach it is essential to consider the nature of the evidence upon which it is based, and as far as it is possible to determine the theory appears to stem exclusively from adolescent patients whom Erikson has seen himself or heard about from others. As he writes when discussing identity diffusion (1969, p. 25):

> The sources at my disposal are the case histories of a number of young patients who sought treatment following an acutely disturbed period between the ages of sixteen and twenty-four. A few were seen, and fewer treated, by me personally . . . the largest number are former patients now on record in the files of the Austen Riggs Center. . . . The fact that the cases known to me were seen in a private institution in the Berkshires, and at a public clinic in industrial Pittsburgh, suggests that at least the two extremes of socio-economic status in the U.S. (and thus two extreme forms of identity problems) are represented here. . . . Whether, and in what way, disturbances such as are outlined here also characterize those more completely placed somewhere near the middle of the socio-economic ladder, remains, at this time, an open question.

Thus there is little to show that in his thinking Erikson gives consideration to the course of normal adolescent development, for apart from his clinical work his interests lie chiefly in anthropological findings (*Childhood and Society*) and in the study of historical characters such as Maxim Gorky and Martin Luther (*Young Man Luther*). The impression has been fostered of adolescence, particularly late adolescence, as a time of marked disturbance in identity, but it is obvious that very much more evidence is needed before such notions are more than important possibilities.

In the present context especial interest is attached to the developmental aspects of self-image in adolescence. While there is in the literature some excellent work, which has already been mentioned, on the adolescent self-image at one particular age (Rosenberg, 1965), it is remarkable that there have been so few developmental studies, and unfortunate that what limited evidence there is does nothing to clarify matters.

One of the earliest studies was that of Engel (1959), who used a Q-sort technique for the assessment of the adolescent's self-concept. She administered the test to boys and girls in the eighth (thirteen years) and tenth (fifteen years) grades in the USA, and then two years later to the same groups who were by then in the tenth and twelfth grades. Engel found a relative stability of self-concept between thirteen and fifteen, and fifteen and seventeen, which was demonstrated by an overall item-by-item correlation of ·53 between first and second testing with an instrument of which the test-retest reliability over ten days was ·68. She also found, interestingly, that those subjects whose self-concept on first testing was negative were significantly less stable in their self-concept than were those whose initial self-concept was positive. Furthermore those who persisted in a negative self-concept showed significantly more maladjustment on the MMPI than those who persisted in a positive self-concept. Unfortunately no evidence is given regarding sex differences.

Carlson (1965) refers directly to Engel's study, pointing out the need for a further investigation of the evidence indicating that self-image remains stable during adolescence. Unfortunately, though, having pointed this out, Carlson goes on to investigate something rather different, for here the research involved a very small sample (thirty-three girls and sixteen boys) which was followed up longitudinally over a six-year period. The children were first tested at twelve years of age, and then again at eighteen, by means of a self-descriptive questionnaire from which was derived, (1) social orientation, (2) personal orientation, and (3) self-esteem. This last was defined as the congruence between self and ideal-self descriptions. The results showed that while at twelve years there were no differences between boys and girls on social and personal orientation, by eighteen girls were significantly more socially oriented and boys significantly more personally oriented. Results also showed that median self-esteem scores remained identical, for both boys and girls, from twelve to eighteen years of age.

Finally, a more recent study by Katz and Zigler (1967) contains results in direct contradiction to Carlson's conclusions. Subjects were sixty boys and sixty girls in the fifth (ten years), eighth (thirteen years) and eleventh (sixteen years) grades, whose real and ideal self-image was assessed both by questionnaire and on an adjective check list. Self-image disparity was defined as the degree of difference between real and ideal self-image, and results showed that self-image disparity increased in a linear fashion with age, with the greatest change occurring between the ten- and thirteen-year levels. Based on these results Katz and Zigler argue that such disparity is an adaptive feature in personality, rather than the opposite, as has usually been assumed. The authors write (1967, p. 194):

> Rather than being ominous in nature, increasing self-image disparity would invariably appear to accompany the attainment of higher levels of development, since the greater cognitive differentiation found at such levels must invariably lead to a greater capacity for self-derogation, guilt and anxiety.

Thus only one study, that of Engel, is directly concerned with self-image *per se*, and the results here indicate some degree of stability between the ages of thirteen and seventeen. Carlson selects personal and social orientation—an aspect of the personality which would seem to be only tenuously related to self-image—and shows that this does change between twelve and eighteen, while with regard to the disparity between real and ideal self-image (what Carlson calls self-esteem) the two studies are in direct contradiction. One possible explanation for this is that what Katz and Zigler pick up between ten and sixteen, Carlson may have missed, since on second testing her subjects were already eighteen. Whatever else is uncertain, however, one thing is quite clear—further investigation of self-image in adolescence is essential, with particular reference to Erikson's notions of identity crisis and identity diffusion.

The evidence
The results pertaining to self-image in the present study are based primarily on two sentences, though the responses to picture 10 will also be discussed in this context. The two sentences are 10 (SOMETIMES WHEN I THINK ABOUT MYSELF . . .) and 14 (NOW AND AGAIN I REALIZE THAT I . . .).

Here again themes have been analysed in terms of whether they reflect constructive or negative attitudes. In this case a Constructive theme would be one which indicated a positive orientation towards the self. Included here are ideas of personal worth, future potential, value to the community or to others, and so on. An example would be 'SOMETIMES WHEN I THINK ABOUT MYSELF I think I am necessary in this world'. Negative themes, on the other hand, are those which reflect a feeling of worthlessness, of insignificance, of inadequacy, or of the general futility of living. An example here would be 'NOW AND AGAIN I REALIZE THAT I am no use to anybody'.

Results derived from sentence 14 are illustrated in figure 3.2 (similar results for sentence 10 may be found in Appendix C). This is a result which is in direct support of Engel's (1959) study discussed above. While her findings illustrated a relative stability of self-concept between the years of thirteen and seventeen, the present study, being a cross-sectional one, illustrates that the proportions in each age group who feel negatively about themselves remain strikingly similar. Furthermore it is of considerable interest to note there are no significant differences between the sexes at any of the age levels, indicating an almost identical development for boys and girls.

There can be little doubt that this evidence is of major importance in relation to Erikson's theory of identity, for it becomes apparent that at no one stage are there signs of a greater degree of disturbance or crisis in self-image than at any other. Even the eleven-year-olds as a group look similar to the seventeen-year-olds. Clearly it cannot be assumed from this evidence that individual adolescents do not experience an identity crisis at some time between the years of eleven and

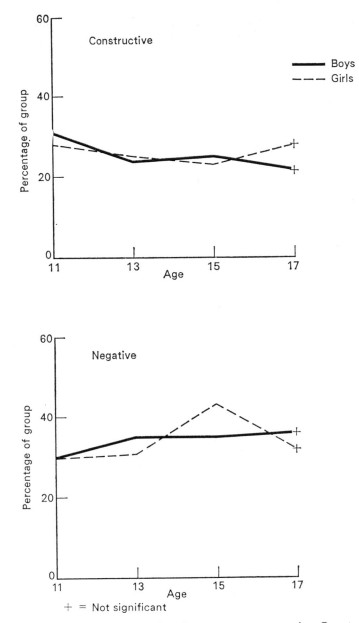

Figure 3.2 *Proportions of each age group expressing Constructive and Negative themes on sentence 14*

seventeen; in fact in view of the proportion of Negative themes at various ages (ranging from 30 per cent to 43 per cent) it seems probable that a considerable number do experience such a feeling. The crucial point, however, is that the older adolescents appear no different from the younger groups; in other words there is no evidence up to the present to show that a developmental phenomenon is involved.

One possibility, however, is that although all age groups express approximately the same proportion of Negative themes, the actual nature of these themes differs from group to group. It was decided therefore to undertake a further analysis of the Negative themes expressed in response to sentences 10 and 14. Such a process indicated that the large majority of Negative responses concerning self-image fall into two categories—those which concentrate on specifically negative personal qualities and those which concern identity—and there appeared to be virtually no differences between age groups in the distribution of these responses. To illustrate this a few of the responses of the youngest and oldest adolescents which fall into the two categories have been selected. For simplicity all have been taken from sentence 14.

PERSONAL QUALITIES

Eleven-year-old boy: 'NOW AND AGAIN I REALIZE THAT I make silly mistakes and make a fool out of myself.'

Eleven-year-old girl: 'NOW AND AGAIN I REALIZE THAT I say too much about my personal life and grumble too much.'

Eleven-year-old girl: 'NOW AND AGAIN I REALIZE THAT I am unnecessarily bossy.'

Eleven-year-old boy: 'NOW AND AGAIN I REALIZE THAT I am a very selfish person.'

Seventeen-year-old boy: 'NOW AND AGAIN I REALIZE THAT I am a real fool.'

Eighteen-year-old boy: 'NOW AND AGAIN I REALIZE THAT I am a pretty nasty person.'

Seventeen-year-old girl: 'NOW AND AGAIN I REALIZE THAT I am sometimes quite horrible to my friends and especially my mother.'

Seventeen-year-old girl: 'NOW AND AGAIN I REALIZE THAT I am unreasonable.'

IDENTITY

Twelve-year-old girl: 'NOW AND AGAIN I REALIZE THAT I am not the person I seem to be.'

Eleven-year-old girl: 'NOW AND AGAIN I REALIZE THAT I wish I had a different personality.'

Eleven-year-old boy: 'NOW AND AGAIN I REALIZE THAT I am nothing but a small puny little boy in this world.'

Twelve-year-old boy: 'NOW AND AGAIN I REALIZE THAT I do not like me.'

Seventeen-year-old girl: 'NOW AND AGAIN I REALIZE THAT I am very confused about many things.'

Seventeen-year-old girl: 'NOW AND AGAIN I REALIZE THAT I am the most insignificant person in my world and therefore *the world* and then I feel like giving up.'

Seventeen-year-old boy: 'NOW AND AGAIN I REALIZE THAT I would have liked to have taken a different course from the one I am travelling now.'

Seventeen-year-old boy: 'NOW AND AGAIN I REALIZE THAT I am totally unimportant and would like to start my life all over again.'

From this evidence it may be seen that almost exactly similar themes are being expressed by those at both ends of the age spectrum, indicating that much the same issues preoccupy adolescents at all levels. Apart from this evidence, though, the fact that individual teenagers struggle at times with identity problems is only too well illustrated by a further look at some of the qualitative material in the shape of two rather unusual stories, the first slightly zany, the second definitely disturbing.

PICTURE 6.   THIRTEEN-YEAR-OLD BOY

'People always seem to avoid me' he mumbled. 'You would think I wasn't like them.' He could hear them mutter something then laugh. It was hard to keep on walking as if you didn't hear them, although you knew

they were laughing at you. 'Prejudice is a totally un-
warranted attitude' he continued to himself. 'It really is
a strange emotion' he pondered, scratching his purple hair
thoughtfully.

PICTURE 4.   FIFTEEN-YEAR-OLD GIRL

This suggests to me a person who is a drop out of society.
The other group conform and lead very narrow lives. He
has other ideas he thinks why should I conform he leads a
very different life to them. He has very different ideas and
he dresses differently and behaves in such a way that they
call him mad. He dresses the way he feels, he behaves the
way he wants to at any time of day. If he wants to dance
all the way down London Rd. he will. He does not bother
what people say to him or about him. He is very musical
and imaginative. This person leads a very different life he
cannot understand himself. He will die early. He puts a
false act on with his friends. He is too inward.

In spite of all this, there clearly remains a major problem.
On the one hand Erikson suggests the existence of an identity
crisis among older adolescents. On the other hand the empirical
findings show no evidence of a developmental phenomenon,
although evidently a minority at all age levels appear to be
struggling with this issue. Perhaps one of the difficulties here
is that of definition. Douvan and Adelson point out the ambiguous nature of the term identity when they write (1966, p. 15):
'Technically speaking the identity concept is not altogether
satisfactory; since it is allusive, complex and connotative. Its
connotativeness is explicitly recognized by Erikson who prefers
to let the term "identity" speak for itself in a number of
connotations.'

Furthermore it will have been noticed that just these problems have been illustrated in the present context. It has been
necessary to use the term 'self-image' to identify a general
theme, but in the analysis of the material a further distinction
has had to be made between specific personal qualities and a
broader notion of 'identity'. In fact it is probable that Erikson's
use of identity is roughly synonymous with the use of self-image
here—generally speaking it is that area covered by answers to

questions such as 'Who am I?' or 'What sort of a person am I?'

As it happens Douvan and Adelson, having drawn attention to a part of the puzzle, also provide a clue to the solution. They argue that in adolescence two types of identity problem may be distinguished—those concerned with present identity, and those concerned with future identity: 'The normal adolescent holds, we think, two conceptions of himself—what he is, and what he will be' (1966, p. 23).

It will be argued here that the dilemma posed by Erikson's theory and the empirical evidence may be solved by considering that issues surrounding present identity are manifested by a minority throughout the age range while conflicts over future identity do indeed increase with age. In order to explore this further, the data from picture 10 must now be considered. This is a picture showing a young person perched on a windowsill, and while it is not clear whether the individual is coming in or going out, it is most often seen as someone on the threshold of an experience, often facing towards the future. Here themes have been scored as Constructive where action or behaviour is straightforward, with no conflict involved. For example:

It is night and a boy has opened his bedroom window to get out of the house without risking meeting this parents. He lives in a bungalow so he can slip out easily. He wants to meet a girl and to talk to her privately. He does this and it leads to his engagement to her.

On the other hand Negative themes are those in which some difficulty or conflict arises, for example:

This boy has just returned from a night with his girl-friend. His parents don't approve of her and so he has to do it secretly. He left a dummy in his bed but is about to receive a terrible shock. His parents have found him out and removed the dummy. On his pillow is a note to say, 'We are waiting up for you, come in to our bedroom on your return'. With a fast beating heart he enters his parents' room.

It will be seen from figure 3.3. that, while there are no significant differences between age groups for Constructive themes, the Negative themes increase significantly with age, and that this trend is similar for both boys and girls.

In view of the fact that there were no differences between age

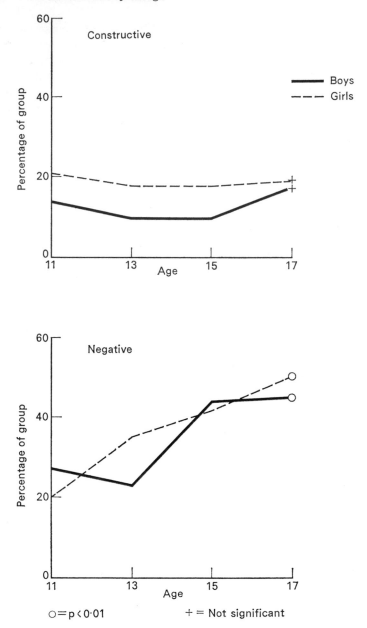

Figure 3.3 *Proportions of each age group expressing Constructive and Negative themes on picture 10*

groups where the earlier results were concerned it seemed necessary to look more closely at the nature of the conflicts which are increasing with age. To this end a distinction was made between External conflict, where the conflict was between an individual and authority figures of one sort or another (parents, teachers, police and so on), an example of which would be the story quoted above, and Internal conflict, where the conflicting forces lie within the individual. For example:

This is the escape. The person is just about to leave the 'darkness' for good and he is having second thoughts as to whether he is making the right decision.

In table 3.1 the proportions of the two types of Negative theme in each age group are set out, and it will be seen that for both boys and girls the number of External conflicts decreases with age, with a concomitant increase in the proportions who express themes of Internal conflict. Furthermore it is apparent that the proportions for boys at all ages are similar to the proportions for girls who are two years younger; in other words seventeen-year-old boys show a similar distribution of Internal and External conflicts as do fifteen-year-old girls.

Table 3.1 *The proportions of External and Internal conflicts at each age level among those who express Negative themes on picture 10*

Age	External conflict	Internal conflict	N
	%	%	
	Boys		
11	64	36	27
13	50	50	26
15	43	57	37
17	33	67	34
	Girls		
11	52	48	18
13	42	58	35
15	33	67	41
17	25	75	37

.These results do illustrate a developmental trend, unlike the evidence from the sentences discussed earlier, and it has been suggested that the explanation for this lies in the distinction between present and future identity. The sentence-completion test asks questions of the 'Who are you?' variety. When someone responds to 'NOW AND AGAIN I REALIZE THAT I . . .' or to 'SOMETIMES WHEN I THINK ABOUT MYSELF I . . . ' they will be responding by and large with some view of themselves as they are at present. It appears however that picture 10 has elicited a rather different aspect of identity. What has been classified as Internal conflict turns out to be a concern with the future. Not 'Who am I?' but 'Who will I become?', 'What am I going to do?', 'What does the future hold?' It is to these questions that the stories on picture 10 are primarily addressed, as a few examples will illustrate.

SEVENTEEN-YEAR-OLD GIRL

His mind was troubled, he did not know which way to turn. Could he forget his past and that terrible imprisonment he had suffered. He looked out of his window and saw air, freedom—yes, freedom different than he had seen for many months. He wondered whether the fears and difficulties which had obsessed him then would ever free his mind, or whether he would for ever be haunted by them. Turning back to his room he saw how different everything was. He now was among his own people, his family, his friends but how distant he seemed from them. He once more went to bed and tried to sleep.

FIFTEEN-YEAR-OLD GIRL

I've often tried to wander through thought and space of time. I wanted to penetrate the deep feeling of my mind. The significance of its being. I tried and tried to look through the windows of my mind to see what's there, realy. To grasp the real meaning of life. In fact to look into the windows of the world. Until one day I heard a fragment of a song, 'passing from dawn to eternity, I want to be, in the warm hold of your loving mind' then I new, it was Patsy, my lover; the window opened and I found my way.

SEVENTEEN-YEAR-OLD GIRL

Paul's life was in a mess, so he thought, he needed to escape, or just to sort out his confused ideas about life. One dark night he opened his window and looked out. He had been doing a great deal of thinking all that night. Suddenly he saw what he had been searching for, his purpose in life. He knew he could not have thought it out for himself. Somewhere out there in the night there was a God or someone like a god that had helped him, if only he knew.

SEVENTEEN-YEAR-OLD BOY

A schoolboy again, trying to escape from the darkness of the institution that he hates. The window—its light— represents freedom to him. Once he has climbed through it he can live again. His face appears to be frenzied as he climbs to his freedom. Will he obtain his goal? Impossible to really say, but one doesn't think so. The 'darkness' seems to have too great a hold on him. This place doesn't of course have to be a school. It could represent any worries, or things that are oppressing him. The meaning of the window, however remains unchanged.

EIGHTEEN-YEAR-OLD BOY

I can see myself not really knowing what to do. I can see a bright future if I can just get away from the limiting influence of school. I can also see myself trying to decide what goes on after life, and whether it is worthwhile trying to take the plunge and find out. The window is open and the opportunity is there—I have a good education, a good home—what will I make of them? I wish I could see right out of that window into my future.

Thus the possibility of a solution to the paradox concerning self-image has been suggested. A proportion of responses at each age level, though not a large one, reflects some aspect of a negative self-image. This may be in terms of specific personal qualities, or it may be to do with broader identity issues, such as personal insignificance. This finding is in line with most previous studies which found no developmental change in self-image during adolescence. On the other hand anxiety over future identity does increase with age. This is consistent with Douvan and Adelson's point of view, and in addition it fills out Erikson's picture of the ego task of 'identity versus identity diffusion' which up to now has been based entirely on an atypical and disturbed population.

4

Heterosexual relationships

Nowhere is adolescent change more striking than in the area of heterosexual relationships, a fact which is clearly illustrated by a comparison between the pre-adolescent lack of interest in, or even antipathy to, the opposite sex and the stage six or seven years later when a permanent or stable relationship is often the individual's most pressing concern. Both the magnitude and the psychological implications of this upheaval within the adolescent are sometimes in danger of being forgotten, and it will be the purpose of this chapter to examine some of the changes which are concomitant with such a process, and to look in particular at the similarities and differences between boys and girls with regard to this aspect of their development.

In reviewing the literature on heterosexual relationships in adolescence both the evidence regarding actual behaviour and that concerning attitudes and conflicts must be considered. To begin with the behavioural aspects, there is no doubt that the most important and extensive work in this area is Schofield's report entitled *The Sexual Behaviour of Young People* (1965). Evidence was based on carefully designed interviews with a large sample of both boys and girls in the age range fifteen to nineteen. While the book contains a large amount of primary information, in general the approach taken is not a developmental one, and thus in a number of crucial areas no information is provided on age changes. One exception to this is in the consideration of the incidence of sexual activity. Here an excellent picture has been obtained of the relation between age and various forms of sexual behaviour, with evidence showing, for example, that many more girls than boys are dating in the younger age group (fifteen to seventeen) while in the older group (seventeen to nineteen) the boys appear to have caught up and to be at approximately the same level as the girls. Another facet of this evidence is that girls appear to show no change in the level of dating behaviour between sixteen and eighteen, whereas boys show a very significant change between these two ages.

In a number of other studies (e.g. Burchinal, 1964; Willmott, 1966; Douvan and Adelson, 1966) adolescents have also been asked directly about the nature of their relationships with the opposite sex at various periods, and not surprisingly all studies show an increase in stable relationships with age. Typical results, in this case for working-class boys, are illustrated in table 4.1 from Willmott (1966, p. 44):

Table 4.1 *The incidence, for boys, of various self-reported relationships with girls*

	14–15	16–18	19–20
	%	%	%
'Have little to do with girls' 'See girls around'	58	33	20
'Take girls out sometimes'	24	41	24
'Regular girlfriend, engaged or married'	18	26	56

Such a table shows clearly the developmental nature of heterosexual relationships in adolescence, with the expected decrease in avoidance and concomitant increase in stability of interaction. The relatively high incidence of casual relationships in middle adolescence is worth noting, and seems likely to be related to initial anxieties concerning dating and involvement. However a further issue here, and one over which there is some controversy, is the question of the time at which stable relationships first occur. Burchinal (1964) provides the most coherent picture, and argues that there is little difference between the sexes in this respect. He points to a considerable amount of evidence which shows that both boys and girls begin to date or go steady at the same time, and he gives median ages for initial dating in America as between 14·1 and 14·9 years. He writes (p. 199): 'dating is a social relationship which is defined by cultural norms, not by biological development *per se.*' This implies, of course, a clear distinction between physical sexual development and overt behaviour.

It is unfortunate that corroborative evidence is not available in Schofield's work as the lower end of his age range is fifteen, but his subjects were asked in retrospect the age at which they started kissing. Interestingly there are virtually no differences between the proportion of boys and girls reporting this at thirteen and fourteen (1965, pp. 33 and 34). However the biggest differences between boys and girls in kissing behaviour appear to be at fifteen and sixteen, with a higher proportion of girls reporting this behaviour, which fits closely with the evidence on dating mentioned earlier.

Turning now to the question of attitudes and conflicts, consideration must be given to two important studies, those of Douvan and Adelson (1966) and of Powell (1955) both of which have already been mentioned. The evidence of the former is based on interviews with girls of three age groups—those of under fourteen (N = 844), fourteen to sixteen (N = 822) and seventeen to eighteen (N = 259). From the interview material Douvan and Adelson build up a picture of the pre-adolescent girl as someone who treats dating rather as an intellectual issue, giving no real indication of emotional involvement with boys. At this stage, it is argued, heterosexual relationships appear to be marked by superficiality, with girls remaining relatively unaware of the emotional bases of such relationships. This superficiality is illustrated by their concern with appearances illustrated in table 4.2, taken from Douvan and Adelson (1966, p. 402).

With regard to the fourteen- to sixteen-year group Douvan and Adelson propose that they are very much involved in starting their 'dating careers', that they have considerable anxieties about this, and that therefore they take a 'defensive rather than interactive stance *vis-à-vis* boys'. Much of the evidence for this defensiveness comes from the girls' reactions to imaginary situations; for example 'What should a girl do if her

fiancé asks her to change certain habits and manners?' A girl
in this age group, according to Douvan and Adelson, sees this as a
criticism, and treats it as a threat to her integrity, tending to
react aggressively by breaking off the relationship.

Only in late adolescence, in the seventeen- to eighteen-year
age range, as the initial anxieties subside, do girls begin to
interact fully with boys, and to bring understanding and emotional awareness to heterosexual relationships. Evidence for
this may be found in the increasing expression of the need for
sensitivity, as shown in table 4.2.

Table 4.2 *Answers to question—'What to you think makes
a girl popular with boys?'*

	Under 14	*14–16*	*17–18*
	%	%	%
Appearance	56	39	38
Good personality	25	47	48
Sensitivity	28	33	41
Morality	7	9	10

The second study, that of Powell, approaches heterosexual
relationships from a different angle altogether, using an unusual
and original method. The study is in fact concerned not only
with relationships between boys and girls but also with other
relevant areas of adolescent functioning which will be discussed
in the appropriate chapters. Subjects were 224 boys and an
equal number of girls ranging in age from ten to thirty years.
A word association test was used, in which were included words
relating to, among other areas, heterosexual relationships (e.g.
dance, kissing, dates, etc.). A set of neutral words was also included, and the mean differences in reaction times to the critical
and the neutral words were used as indices of conflict; in other
words the greater the difference between reaction times to, say,
the heterosexual words and the neutral words, the greater the
conflict surrounding heterosexuality. The findings of this study
are particularly important as a result of the manner in which
they illustrate combined developmental and sex differences.

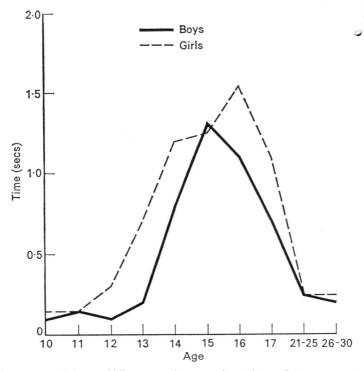

Figure 4.1 *Mean differences in reaction times between neutral and 'heterosexual' words on a word association test (after Powell, 1955)*

It can be seen from the graph that conflict as defined and measured in this study occurs earlier for girls than for boys, differences being statistically significant at twelve and thirteen. In addition conflict continues at a higher level for a longer period of time for girls than for boys, the only age at which boys show minimally more conflict than girls being at fifteen.

In summarizing the findings so far, it is possible to abstract a number of relatively well-supported facts concerning the adolescents' heterosexual relationships. These are, first, that for both boys and girls there is an increase with age in stable relationships; second, that the number of both boys and girls having casual short-term relationships is highest in middle adolescence; third, that the level of anxiety is also highest, for boys and girls, in middle adolescence, and not at puberty as might be expected. On the other hand when one turns to the question of sex differences there is a very much greater degree of uncertainty. Both Schofield and Burchinal indicate that there are no sex differences in early adolescence, the former in addition showing that what differences there are in dating behaviour occur in middle adolescence. On the other hand Powell, in his consideration of anxiety, indicates that the significant differences between boys and girls are precisely in early adolescence, at twelve and thirteen, though his results also illustrate a marked though not statistically significant difference at sixteen.

With these issues in mind, consideration may now be given to the present findings. Particular attention will need to be paid to the question of sex differences, especially in early adolescence, as well as to the theme of anxiety in heterosexual development. In the studies reviewed no mention has been made of anxiety or antipathy to the opposite sex in early adolescence, and what results there are point to anxiety in the middle period. It will be important to explore this issue further, and to see what evidence there is for the various psychological aspects of sexual maturation which have been proposed.

The evidence

The results in this chapter are derived from two pictures—no. 2 and no. 9, and two sentences—no. 6 (A BOY AND A GIRL TO-GETHER . . . or A GIRL AND A BOY TOGETHER . . .) and no. 11 (FOR A BOY GIRLS . . . or FOR A GIRL BOYS . . .). Again stories and sentences have been scored for Constructive and Negative themes, and in figure 4.2 the relationship between age and the expression of these themes is illustrated for sentence 11.

From this it is evident that for both boys and girls Constructive themes increase up to the age of fifteen, after which there is either a plateau, or a small decrease. Results from other sources, such as picture 2 and sentence 6, support this finding, corroborating also the lack of any striking sex differences. Where the expression of Negative themes is concerned, however, quite a different picture emerges. Here the incidence of such themes decreases with age for boys, having started at quite a high level. Girls, on the other hand, start at a lower level, decrease till fifteen, but then show a fairly sharp increase. At

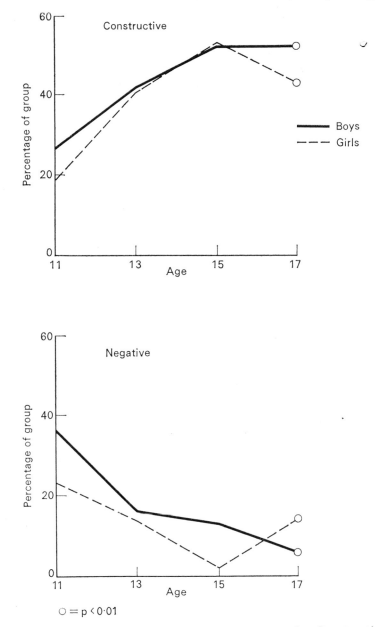

Figure 4.2 *Proportions of each age group expressing Constructive and Negative themes on sentence 11*

both eleven and fifteen the difference between boys and girls is statistically significant, boys expressing a greater proportion of Negative themes.

Before an explanation is sought for these results some idea of the quality of the Negative responses may be illustrated by the following examples from eleven- and twelve-year-old boys, some of which have, apart from their intrinsic interest, an undoubted charm:

Eleven-year-old boy: 'FOR A BOY GIRLS are utter menaces.'

Eleven-year-old boy: 'FOR A BOY GIRLS are a nuisance because they remind you of things you must not do.'

Eleven-year-old boy: 'FOR A BOY GIRLS are pretty though it isn't fun to play with their dolls.'

Twelve-year-old boy: 'FOR A BOY GIRLS are friends who will help but when they are treated badly they sometimes turn nasty.'

Twelve-year-old boy: 'FOR A BOY GIRLS are his enemy sometimes, as they poke fun at him.'

Eleven-year-old boy: 'A BOY AND A GIRL TOGETHER can be very embarrassing.'

Much the same type of material may be found amongst the girls' responses:

Eleven-year-old girl: 'FOR A GIRL BOYS are very stupid and not needed.'

Eleven-year-old girl: 'FOR A GIRL BOYS are something that kicks and punches.'

Eleven-year-old girl: 'FOR A GIRL BOYS games are rather stupid.'

Thirteen-year-old girl: 'FOR A GIRL BOYS are sometimes quite frightening and difficult to understand.'

In these responses a number of conventional reasons are given for the antipathy: embarrassment, anxiety and uncertainty about the reactions of the opposite sex, sensitivity with regard to mockery, or just plain dislike of other types of activity. However these are clearly only symptoms. When writing of masculine sexual development Blos states (1965, p. 147): 'The most remarkable observation about the pre-adolescent boy is his decisive turning away from the opposite sex as soon as the first strivings of puberty increase drive pressure and upset the balance between ego and id . . . .'

It will be noted that such an explanation is very similar to the one discussed in the previous chapter concerning solitude. Because of the upsurge of instincts at puberty self-control becomes a problem. This leads to anxiety, and thence to a wish to avoid the anxiety-arousing situation. Such an explanation would certainly be entirely consistent with the present finding of a high proportion of Negative themes expressed in reaction to heterosexual situations in early adolescence, and would be further corroborated by the parallel sex differences found in both cases. To solitude and heterosexual relationships, eleven-year-old boys express a higher proportion of Negative themes than do girls, indicating the probability that there is a similar underlying cause for both results.

One further finding which needs some explanation is the increase among the older girls of the expression of Negative themes. A seventeen-year-old girl herself makes a start in this direction when she writes: 'FOR A GIRL BOYS are fun at thirteen but a worry at nineteen.'

If it is remembered that most of the girls in this sample are from grammar schools, and that for many of them therefore academic performance at seventeen and eighteen is extremely important, then it is not surprising that a small proportion begin once again to feel negatively about boys.

Two significant points remain. First, the discussion has concentrated on Negative themes, whereas in fact a far greater proportion of adolescents express Constructive themes in response to heterosexual situations. Two endearing responses may serve as reminders of this fact:

Seventeen-year-old boy: 'FOR A BOY GIRLS are sacred grails.'
Seventeen-year-old girl: 'FOR A GIRL BOYS are the cause of the most ecstatic and most tragic moments in her life.'

In addition one young boy gets as close as anyone can do to providing a developmental perspective on heterosexual relationships from his vantage point.

Thirteen-year-old boy: 'FOR A BOY GIRLS are (1) 1–11 disinterest-
ing (2) 11–18 interesting (3) 19–21 very interesting (4) 21–80
wifes.'

The second point of importance is that while reference has
been made to anxiety at eleven and at seventeen, nothing has
been said of anxiety in middle adolescence. On the other hand,
in reviewing the literature it was noted that almost all mention
of anxiety was restricted to just this period—the fourteen-,
fifteen- and sixteen-year stage. It is an indisputable fact that in
the quantitative results presented here Negative themes are at
their lowest and Constructive themes at their highest in middle
adolescence. This is not to say, however, that anxiety is absent.
Rather it seems probable that in this study a relatively deeper
level of anxiety is being tapped, while the more behavioural
uncertainty referred to in other studies is masked by the nature
of the present enquiry. None the less even here a minority
certainly do express a striking range of anxieties connected with
sexual relationships, and an examination of a small selection of
stories, set out in developmental sequence, will illustrate some
of these.

Among the younger age groups there are two particular
themes of note, the first of these being the experience of sex as
an onlooker.

PICTURE 9.   ELEVEN-YEAR-OLD GIRL
They stood under the tree in the moonlight, my sister and
'Him'. She seems to dream all the time she put salt in her
tea, milk on her toast jam on her cereal. But tonight under
that tree they just stand there just looking never saying
anything. What am I to do, 'Oh Sister!'

PICTURE 2.   THIRTEEN-YEAR-OLD BOY
There they were standing in the back garden and I felt
hatred for him because I was jealous. I could hardly bear
to look when they started to kiss I felt like shooting him
down with a gun or drowning him in a pond. The hills
reached up towards the sky the moon was looking sadly
down at me I felt like crying.

PICTURE 6. THIRTEEN-YEAR-OLD BOY

The two men were standing in the queue waiting to see a
sex film which was uncensored and considered absolutely
disgusting by many people of a higher intellect. The third
man stood watching them disgusted that they should want
to see 'such slander and mis-use of film to such an extent'
He walked off down the road.

The second feature of note among the younger groups is a
remarkable capacity for denial, which is particularly well illustrated in the following two stories:

PICTURE 10. ELEVEN-YEAR-OLD BOY

The picture looks as if its a carry-on from the last one. It
was too cold to stay out for the night so the boy has just
climbed up a drainpipe and has got into his bedroom. The
girl cannot go home so the boy will let the girl sleep with
him in his bedroom since it is a small house and there is
not a guestroom.

PICTURE 10. ELEVEN-YEAR-OLD GIRL

It is Michael Groves in the picture and as usual on his
nightly rounds going to all girls houses at night to kiss and
hold and cuddle all his girls. When he wakes up in the
morning he is as timid as a mouse he doesn't know what
he did. He always waits till midnight and all his girls are
in bed asleep and then he creeps about.

It is in looking at the stories of slightly older adolescents that
the most overt references to anxiety are to be found. At this
time it is natural to discover an increasing number who are
actually participating in heterosexual relationships, but with
this comes worry, fear or guilt, all inevitable consequences of
becoming involved in something which is in some senses forbidden and in many ways unknown. It is not surprising, therefore, to find that a proportion of the stories reflect these feelings.
Perhaps in developmental terms the earliest of these is the fear
of actual rejection or punishment.

PICTURE 2. THIRTEEN-YEAR-OLD GIRL

These are lovers who are going to elope. The house is

where the girl lives, and her parents don't like the man so she is going to run away with him into the hills. They will go away and for a few months they will have a lovely time walking around in the hills and then it will be winter and it will snow and they will both die. Their bodies will be recovered, but nobody will want them anymore.

PICTURE 2.   FIFTEEN-YEAR-OLD GIRL
A couple, Simon and his girlfriend Clare, were newly married and very poor. They had managed to rent a room on the top floor of an old house on the edge of the town. Simon found himself a job and although the money was poor they had just about been able to pay their rent and feed themselves. Then Simon lost his job and Clare being pregnant couldn't work. That was a week ago. They left their room in the middle of the night owing a weeks rent. They found another flat but had to leave it as well, owing rent. In the end they were caught and punished.

There are, of course, other types of 'punishment', and the two stories below illustrate a fear of retribution which no doubt has its roots in early childhood fantasies. In the girl's case it is expressed as follows:

PICTURE 8.   THIRTEEN-YEAR-OLD GIRL
These are the steps of a huge hospital in America. Gathered round the bottom are newspaper men, camera men all waiting for an interview with this incredible woman who is slowly walking down the steps. She is incredible because she has just had twelve babies. All surviving. She feels very ill and walks slowly. When she finally reaches the bottom she collapses and dies.

For the boy, a similar type of fear is barely disguised in this reference to castration:

PICTURE 10.   SEVENTEEN-YEAR-OLD BOY
The man has just finished having it with his bird and will have to watch his penis on the window-sill. His bird loved it. Better than marriage because if her old man had

walked in she would be thrown out. The man has her knickers in his pocket to show his mates. In the end he will have to marry her or go to sea.

To continue with the issue of fears and anxieties, a slightly different theme is that of control—the fear that one will lose control, and the frightening consequences if impulses are allowed expression. For girls this seems to be expressed in the fear of what boys might do.

PICTURE 8.   FIFTEEN-YEAR-OLD GIRL

A gang of boys were waiting in the dark for any girl to come along and two came round the corner they jumped them. They had been waiting for this, a chance to rape any unsuspecting girl, the struggle for freedom was hard but at last a law car was seen and big Joe said 'Clear out, come on run'. They all scattered the police came over to investigate the girls still screaming were helped into a Panda car and taken to hospital. Neither of them could say much as the incident made them mentally ill.

On the other hand for boys the problem of control is expressed in terms of the possible effects of their own behaviour.

PICTURE 4.   SEVENTEEN-YEAR-OLD BOY

The girl is an individual and here stands apart from a group of boys. The boys look upon her as an idle, she is beautiful but cruel. The boys are discussing here and she is just parading in front of them, the boys are shy or ashamed and group together partially out of sight behind the arches. They eventually murder here by mistake in their attempts to have her for themselves.

Not all the stories concerning control have such a pessimistic tone though, and the following one is an example of the realization that control can be lost without such disastrous consequences:

PICTURE 9.   SEVENTEEN-YEAR-OLD BOY

Dark and damp. Two figures huddled together beneath a

tree. Away, but only just, from bustling society, just for a
while. Secretly they had longed for this, now the chance
had come. The boat mustn't be missed. Now . . . now was
the time. Let's live for the present forget the past and
look forward to the future. Here beneath a small tree, all
could (well, not quite all) be revealed. Secret long hidden
desires could come to the boil. God, who cares what anyone
else thinks, let's . . . Let's . . . we must, we need each other
to much . . . it spiralled.'

Finally two stories exemplify the realization on the part of
some of the older adolescents that it is precisely a relationship
with someone of the opposite sex which can give them the
security and stability they need to face the future.

PICTURE IO. SIXTEEN-YEAR-OLD GIRL
It's a boy who wants desperately to see his girl-friend.
She was involved in a car accident and he happened to be
the driver. She was on the critical list and no one was
allowed to see her. He went to see her parents but they
wouldn't have anything to do with him. When she was a
bit better he tried to see her but they kept him out, so he
decided to wait till dark and then climb through the
window. She was so pleased to see him that it gave her
fresh hope, and she wanted to live for him.

PICTURE 2. SEVENTEEN-YEAR-OLD GIRL
In this picture there are a boy and a girl who are talking
together about their future. They can either venture into
the unknown by leaving their families, or they can live as
their parents before them in an ordinary house. The way
is open for them to leave but should they go? I think they
will leave home secure in their love for each other, leaving
the known happiness for the unknown trials and tribula-
tions of a new life.

Thus the stories illustrate the actual quality of the anxieties
and defences which surround heterosexual relationships. It may
seem strange that nothing has been said of homosexuality, but
the simple reason for this is that not more than a handful of

individuals mentioned the subject. This may well be because of the taboos surrounding the topic, or alternatively the nature of the stimuli themselves may have militated against the expression of homosexual themes. In any event, this is ground left uncovered in the present study. On the other hand, issues surrounding both sex differences and the developmental nature of anxiety have been thoroughly discussed. From the evidence one must conclude, with Powell, that there are fairly important differences between boys and girls in early adolescence, particularly with respect to the level of negativism and antipathy towards the opposite sex. As far as Constructive themes are concerned they appear to reach their peak at fifteen or seventeen, just as would have been expected from previous studies. Finally, only qualitative evidence has been produced for the existence of anxiety in middle adolescence. This is not in any way to argue that such anxiety does not exist at this time. Rather, the present study has identified a deeper level of anxiety at an earlier stage, and has elucidated both in quantitative and qualitative terms the nature of the 'turning away' from the opposite sex at puberty described by psychoanalytic writers.

5

Parental relationships

It is possible that adolescence may in some senses be effectively defined by the progress which is made in the relationship between the young person and his parents. Such a relationship is a dynamic, continually changing one, and the adjustments that each makes to accommodate the changes will play a critical part in determining the adolescent's development. A considerable part of the theory pertaining to this relationship stems from the psychoanalytic viewpoint, already considered in previous chapters. Briefly, the theory proposes that the changes at puberty involve the whole of the individual's instinctual life, and include the upsurge not only of the sexual instincts, but also of the aggressive ones as well. These changes are seen as being closely related to a need to break off the infantile ties with the parents, a need which is accompanied by a very ambivalent movement towards emotional autonomy. This inevitably leads to a struggle or conflict between parents and adolescent, partly as a result of the adults' unwillingness to let the child go, and partly because of the adolescent's own need to derogate and criticize the adults upon whom he has been dependent and to whom he is still in reality deeply attached.

The psychoanalytic viewpoint does not provide the only way of conceptualizing parental relationships, and other approaches such as role theory have also been discussed. In addition mention has been made of the general controversy surrounding the 'storm and stress' approach, a controversy which bears very closely upon this particular area of adolescent development. With these points in mind two specific questions may be considered. The first concerns the amount of conflict present in parental relationships. Is conflict with parents a *sine qua non* of adolescence? Is it such an important feature that a concept of adolescence would be incomplete without it? Or has it all been greatly exaggerated, the large majority of adolescents experiencing little, if any, direct conflict with their parents? Just how much is there and how widespread is it? That is the first question. The second is closely related, and can best be expressed by asking: 'If conflict exists, what is its focus?' Is it over independence that the major battles are fought, or are there quite different elements involved, such as envy, jealousy or competition? Remarkably little is known of the components of the conflict, and while research has concentrated on such things as approval or disapproval of parental rules, few attempts have been made to explore what it is which lies at the heart of the relationship, what it is which adolescents are really concerned about when they do feel negative and antagonistic towards parents. Thus it is necessary to discover not only how much conflict exists, but, equally important, what the conflict is about and how it is expressed. Before this is done, however, some further consideration of the literature is indicated.

Attention has already been drawn to the large number of writers (such as Offer, 1969; and Bandura, 1972) who have argued that conflict is not a primary feature of adolescence. However it is probably Elizabeth Douvan and her co-workers who have been the most consistent proponents of this point of view. In an important review of theory and research Douvan and Gold (1966, p. 485) have this to say:

> Traditionally the autonomy issue at adolescence has been conceived as a struggle: . . . Let us state at the outset that research findings, by and large, do not support [this] traditional view. In the large scale studies of normal populations, we do not find adolescents clamoring for freedom or for release from unjust constraint. We do not find rebellious resistance to authority as a dominant theme. For the most part, the evidence bespeaks a modal pattern considerably more peaceful than much theory and most social comment would lead us to expect. 'Rebellious youth' and 'the conflict between generations' are phrases that ring; but, so far as we can tell, it is not the ring of truth they carry so much as the beguiling but misleading tone of drama.

Much of the evidence for this statement appears to come from Douvan's own work published in Douvan and Adelson's *The Adolescent Experience* (1966). In this book the majority of the data concern girls only, though there is some information on boys in the fourteen- to sixteen-year age range.

Where girls alone are concerned Douvan and Adelson do provide some evidence to support their contention that 'the normative adolescent tends to avoid overt conflict with his family'. They show, for example, that there are no age changes in the adolescents' views of parents as strict or lenient, and the figures in table 5.1 illustrate clearly both the lack of developmental change and the strikingly low negativism in attitudes to parental rules (1966, p. 388).

Table 5.1 *Proportions of each age group who express different attitudes to parental rules*

	Under 14	14–16	17–18
	%	%	%
Positive attitude to rules	47	54	56
Neutral attitude	46	34	30
Negative attitude	4	7	5

However Douvan and Adelson do not in fact suggest that, even in girls, such conflict does not exist. They point out that their evidence indicates an overall general trend away from total emotional involvement with the family for girls, and they have one particularly interesting finding which relates the need for autonomy and the specific issues over which conflict occurs. In one of the few examples in the literature of this sort of concern, they asked girls at different ages what they most disagreed with their parents about. The results, in their words, 'illustrate an outward arc of conflict' with three quite different peaks, showing that the primary conflict issue is first narcissistic, in middle adolescence interpersonal, and finally concerned with broader social issues. Thus in the 'under fourteen' group clothing and lipstick were the types of issues over which there was most disagreement, in the 'fourteen to sixteen' group dating appeared to be the major issue, while in the oldest group most disagreements centred around ideas and values.

Where they do make some comparison between the sexes, Douvan and Adelson show that, on the whole, girls stay closer to the family than boys do; in the age range where comparable data are available a greater proportion of girls share some leisure activity with the family, and in emotional independence from the family boys appear very considerably in advance of girls. A nice example of this can be seen in the choice of an adult model ('Who would you most like to be like when you grow up?'). If one considers the proportions of each age group who would like to be like the same sex parent, the evidence shows that by sixteen boys as a group are further away from the parent of the same sex than are girls at eighteen, and the authors' general conclusion is that girls continue in a more 'compliant' relationship with parents throughout adolescence, while boys 'seek more actively for independence and self-regulation'.

Thus, although there is some evidence in *The Adolescent Experience* to support the point of view expressed in Gold and Douvan's statement, it is certainly far from being unequivocal. One issue which obviously needs further elucidation is that of sex differences, for it is not at all clear, as an example, whether boys are equally restrained in their attitudes to parental rules as girls appear to be. Furthermore this study provides an excellent illustration of the problems of methodology referred to earlier, since it is impossible to tell to what degree the interview approach has influenced the results. Finally the sampling limitation must be borne in mind. It is a major weakness of the study that only a small number of boys at one stage during adolescence are being compared with a large number of girls throughout the age range, and this must be stressed continually if the results are not to be misleading.

To move to a study using very different methodology, Powell (1955) based his research, as has been mentioned earlier, on a word association technique. He compared the differences in reaction times between neutral words and critical words concerned with various subjects, among which were parent-child relationships (e.g. 'father', 'children', 'home', 'mother', 'parents'). By utilizing these differences he was able to illustrate the relative amounts of conflict at various ages. It could hardly be contested that the data (represented in figure 5.1) indicate, in comparative terms, a degree of conflict during the fifteen-, sixteen- and seventeen-year age range, though it is interesting to see that this conflict is certainly not of the same order as that connected with heterosexual relationships in the same study (see previous chapter).

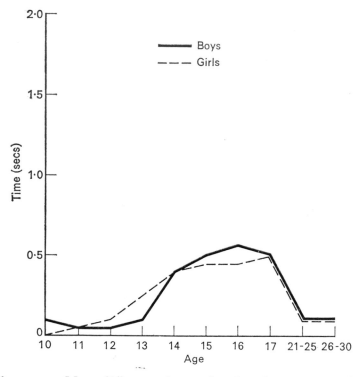

Figure 5.1 *Mean differences in reaction times between neutral and 'parent-child' words on a word association test (after Powell, 1955)*

It will be noted that it is only at thirteen that girls show markedly more conflict than boys, thereafter boys express more conflict than girls up to the post-adolescent period.

Another interesting study showing similar results is that of Liccione (1955). He analysed stories expressed in response to the Thematic Apperception Test by girls of nine, eleven, thirteen, fifteen and seventeen years, and scored the stories for equilibrium or disequilibrium in parental relationships. The results indicated a preponderance of themes of disequilibrium in a ratio of four to one, and also showed that the highest disequilibrium and lowest equilibrium scores occurred almost without exception at the fifteen-year level.

Willmott's (1966) study, one of the few based on a British population, provides further support for the same notion of a peak period in middle to late adolescence. In this work, based on informal interviews with working-class adolescent boys in the East End of London, the sample is divided into three age groups: 14–15, 16–18 and 19–20. Interestingly the data show no change in attitudes to father, but do show a developmental trend in teenagers' attitudes to their mothers. The greatest conflict appeared to be at the sixteen- to eighteen-year level, though it should be added that there was not a lot of conflict at any age. Willmott explains the differences in terms of the remoteness of fathers in the East End, arguing that any negative feelings would be expressed towards the parent who was present and available, i.e. the mother. This finding is noteworthy in view of the fact that working-class boys in the sixteen- to eighteen-year age range would already be out at work, and therefore relatively independent of parents. Thus if conflict was determined by social condition it might be expected to come, for these boys, at an earlier age. That it does not is an indication of the developmental nature of the conflict, and is important in considering the results of the present study.

One other British investigation, that of Musgrove (1964), is of interest because it provides a link between Douvan's position and most of the other studies that have been mentioned. Musgrove used a sentence-completion test to assess both adolescent and adult attitudes, and although unfortunately the age range of the adolescents in the study extended only from eleven to fifteen, there are a number of findings which are relevant in the present context. The author showed first, that within this age range there are no differences between age groups with regard to disapproval of parental rules, and second, that the number of favourable statements concerning the parent of the same sex decreases with age for both boys and girls. Perhaps of greater importance, however, is the finding that adults express a greater degree of hostility towards adolescents than adolescents do to adults, a finding also supported by Eppel and Eppel (1962) and Hess and Goldblatt (1957).

One other question which is closely linked is that concerning changing 'orientation' during adolescence. In addition to his other findings Musgrove also has some information on this, for he asked the children in his sample whom they would most prefer as a companion on an outing. He showed that the critical change occurs between the ages of eleven and thirteen, since over 50 per cent of both boys and girls prefer a parent at eleven, while at thirteen only 13·5 per cent of the boys and 2·1 per cent of the girls choose a parent as a companion. The difference between boys and girls at thirteen is statistically significant.

Bowerman and Kinch (1959) were also interested in this question of family or peer orientation in the USA. In their sample they included approximately 700 boys and girls ranging in age from eleven to fifteen, and a questionnaire was used upon which were based three measures of orientation to family or peers:

(1) the extent to which they were identified with the model;

(2) the extent to which they would prefer to associate with the model;

(3) the extent to which the model had norms and values like their own.

As might be expected the results show a clear shift from family to peer orientation as a function of age on all three measures, but what is most interesting is that the major swing away from the family occurs between thirteen and fourteen for boys, but between twelve and thirteen for girls. Thus the change appears to come one year later for boys than for girls, closely corroborating other evidence discussed above (for example the studies of Powell and Musgrove).

In looking back over these findings three clear trends emerge. First, it seems that the move away from the parents occurs earlier in girls than it does in boys; second, whatever conflict there is between parent and adolescent is greater and lasts longer in boys than in girls; and third, most of the evidence points to a peak age of conflict somewhere in the fifteen- to seventeen-year age range. These three trends are relatively well supported by the studies available, and similar results are to be expected in the present investigation. Apart from these trends, however, a number of uncertainties remain, and in particular it will be noted that neither of the two predominant issues to do with conflict which were identified earlier have been illuminated to any significant degree by the above findings.

Where the amount of conflict is concerned many of the studies indicate a considerable degree of 'difficulty', whether it is defined as disequilibrium, longer reaction times to particular words, or a decrease in the number of favourable statements. On the other hand there is also evidence to show that there is remarkably little criticism of parental rules throughout the age range for girls (Douvan and Adelson), and up to fifteen for boys (Musgrove). It is evident that not only are clearer definitions of conflict required but that also, as has already been mentioned, sex differences and method are variables which may be crucial and cannot be ignored. It seems possible from the evidence that conflict is more likely to be found in boys than in girls, which would explain Douvan's position, and until more is known of the older adolescent boy a fundamental piece of the puzzle is missing, for it has been noted that neither Douvan and Adelson nor Musgrove have evidence on boys above the age of sixteen.

Where the nature of the conflict is concerned there is virtually no evidence available except for that of Douvan and Adelson, who show the typical 'bones of contention' at different ages for girls. This evidence is of great interest, but inevitably raises as many questions as it answers. Apart from the obvious query as to whether there is a similar progression for boys, there is the equally interesting issue of how the adolescent himself views these disagreements. Douvan and Adelson's evidence implies that parental rules are seen as reasonable and just—are these disagreements, then, a product of the unreasonableness of the adolescent? Furthermore we are still far from knowing just how much attachment and independence are at the root of the disagreements. Is this the source of the conflict, or are there others, equally important in determining both content and outcome? With these questions in mind consideration can now be given to the findings of the present research.

The evidence

The evidence with regard to parental relationships is based on two pictures (nos 5 and 7) and on four sentences: no. 1 (USUALLY WHEN A BOY IS WITH HIS MOTHER . . .); no. 4 (FOR A BOY PARENTS . . .); no. 9 (OFTEN A BOY AND HIS FATHER . . .), and no. 13 (WHEN A BOY IS WITH HIS PARENTS . . .). The girls' form of these sentences is set out in Appendix B.

Once again in analysing the imaginative material the initial step has been to distinguish between Constructive and Negative themes. In the case of parental relationships the Constructive category includes themes in which parents are seen as people who can help, who will provide support or security, or with whom it is possible just to enjoy oneself or to have a good time. In other words any material would fall into this category if it implied in one way or another that parents are to be valued. Examples from two of the sentences are: 'FOR A GIRL PARENTS are a shoulder to cry on' and 'WHEN A BOY IS WITH HIS PARENTS he is as proud as he could be'. On the other hand Negative themes are those which in some way reflect the feeling that the relationship is unsatisfactory. Parents are perceived as unhelpful, inhibiting or actually harmful to the individual, ideas which are reflected in the following two examples: 'FOR A BOY PARENTS are too difficult for words' and 'WHEN A GIRL IS WITH HER PARENTS she cannot talk to them'.

The first result is derived from sentence 13.

The data speak for themselves and illustrate a striking developmental pattern. On the one hand boys show a steady decrease in Constructive themes accompanied by a dramatic increase in the expression of Negative themes between the ages of thirteen and seventeen, the peak age for such themes being, as far as it is possible to tell from these results, seventeen. On the other hand girls appear to reach their peak for the expression of Negative themes at fifteen, decreasing thereafter, with a concomitant increase in Constructive themes between fifteen and seventeen. It is especially noteworthy that all three predictions mentioned earlier which can be derived from previous research are borne out by these data. First, girls start the move away from parents earlier than boys (note the large and statistically significant difference in proportions expressing Negative themes

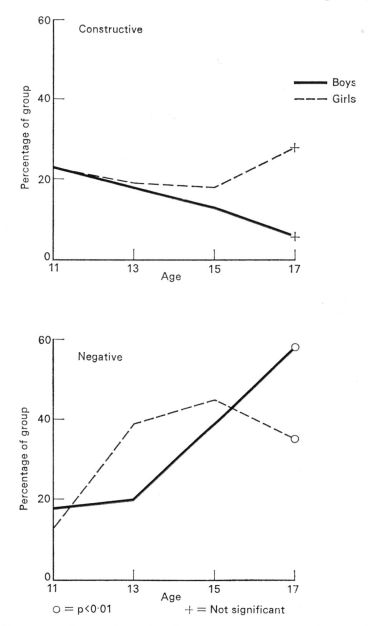

Figure 5.2 *Proportions of each age group expressing Constructive and Negative themes on sentence 13*

at thirteen). Second, the conflict certainly lasts longer for boys than girls, though the relative amount appears to be greater only at seventeen. Third, there is clear evidence that the peak age for conflict is somewhere between fifteen and seventeen.

In view of the remarkable nature of this evidence it will be as well in this case to look closely at other results in the study which might corroborate such a sequence of development. To this end the data from picture 5 are illustrated in figure 5.3.

The picture chosen here is the one closest in content to sentence 13, and once again the graphs need very little commentary or explanation. The similarities are remarkable, and it is perhaps worth noting at this point that the pictures and sentences were completed by almost all the adolescents on separate occasions, thus minimizing any response set. Furthermore the scoring of the responses was carried out by independent judges, none of whom were aware of the sex or age of the subjects whose records they were analysing, nor were they aware of any of the results until all the scoring was completed. Clearly the similarity between the two sets of results provides essential confirmation of these findings which illustrate a fundamental pattern in the development of parental relationships.

It will be noted that the material presented up to this point concerns parents in general. So far no distinction has been made between mothers and fathers. In the sentence-completion test, however, an attempt was made to look a little more closely at the relation between attitude and sex of parent, and some brief mention must be made of these results. (Full details of the actual data may be found in Appendix C.) Essentially the findings show that for boys a similar pattern of development exists, irrespective of whether they respond to mothers, fathers or parents in general; that is to say that as a function of age there is a decrease in Constructive themes and an increase in Negative themes, with the peak expression of these themes occurring always at seventeen. For girls, on the other hand, the pattern is very much more complex. The older the girl, the more likely she is to feel positively about her father, while Negative feelings remain at a low level and show no change with age. Towards the mother, however, the opposite appears to be true—Constructive themes remain stable at a relatively high level between

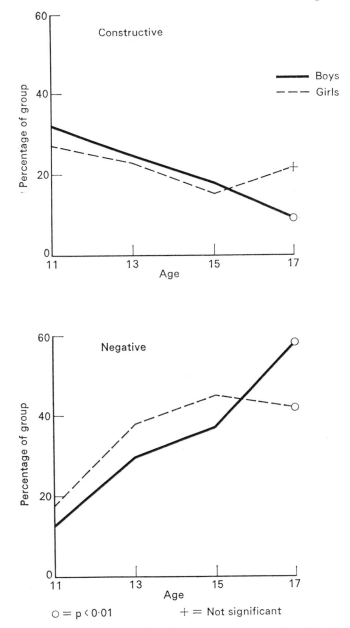

Figure 5.3 *Proportions of each age group expressing Constructive and Negative themes on picture 5*

thirteen and seventeen with, in addition, a significant increase throughout the age range in Negative themes. To summarize, then, while boys differentiate hardly at all according to the sex of the parent, girls appear to be much more sensitive to this factor. With age they show an increasingly positive attitude to fathers, but a complex ambivalent relationship to mothers in which both Constructive and Negative themes are prominent, especially in the older age groups.

A further point of obvious interest is the question of the extent of the conflict. It can be seen from the graphs that to any one item approximately sixty per cent of seventeen-year-old boys express a Negative theme. Is it the same sixty per cent in all cases? And if so, does this mean that the other forty per cent have no negative feelings at all? In order to answer this question, consideration was given to the total number of items in the two tests (six in all) which related to parents, and figure 5.4 shows the number in each age group who express at least one Negative theme on one of the items concerning parents.

Once again the similarity between this and the earlier graphs is striking, and provides further corroboration for the developmental pattern that has already been outlined. However, the main point of the graph is to illustrate the remarkably high percentage of fifteen- and seventeen-year-olds expressing Negative themes—92 per cent of the fifteen-year-old girls and 93 per cent of the seventeen-year-old boys. No-one seeing these figures could have very much doubt that some form of negative attitude towards parents is a significant feature of adolescent development.

Earlier in this chapter the necessity for a clearer definition of conflict was mentioned, and further consideration must now be given to this issue. It could well be, for example, that although approximately the same proportion of fifteen-year-old boys and girls express Negative themes, the nature of the antipathy in the two sexes is quite different. For this reason a further analysis of the themes expressed on sentence 13 was carried out, which indicated approximately five different categories of Negative response. Only two of these, however, differentiate between boys and girls, the two being themes of Frustration, and those which have been entitled 'Feel Different' themes. An example of the former would be 'WHEN A BOY IS WITH HIS PARENTS he feels frustrated, tied down', and of the latter 'WHEN A GIRL IS WITH HER PARENTS she usually is a different person'.

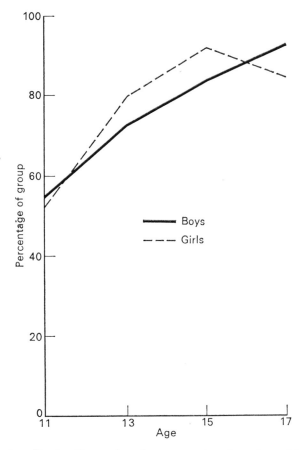

Figure 5.4 *Proportions of each age group expressing at least one Negative theme on those items concerned with parental relationships*

The results, in percentages, are set out in table 5.2.

These results indicate that the content of the Negative responses is not the same for the two sexes. Hardly any boys at any age express Feel Different themes, whereas for the girls' feelings of Frustration are manifestly not an important component of their attitudes towards parents. Of special interest is the fact that the highest proportion of Feel Different themes is expressed by fifteen-year-old girls, while Frustration themes are most common among seventeen-year-old boys. These two ages correspond, of course, to the peak ages for the general expression of Negative themes, indicating the prominent part these two specific issues play in the overall pattern of parental relationships.

Table 5.2   *The proportions of Frustration and Feel Different themes at each age level among those who express Negative responses on sentence 13*

Age	Frustration	Feel Different	N
	%	%	
	Boys		
11	11	0	18
13	26	5	19
15	32	3	31
17	41	10	39
	Girls		
11	0	7	15
13	12	9	43
15	9	40	43
17	8	28	25

There is little need for an explanation of the Frustration theme. It is relatively straightforward, reflecting almost always some form of clash or confrontation, and often referring to specific behavioural constraints. Two interesting examples are:

Seventeen-year-old boy: 'WHEN A BOY IS WITH HIS PARENTS he is usually chained up.'

Seventeen-year-old boy: 'WHEN A BOY IS WITH HIS PARENTS he can experience claustrophobia "cribbed, cabined and confined".'

Where the 'Feel Different' theme is concerned some further comment is necessary since there has been little mention of such a feeling in the literature, and there are some difficulties involved in arriving at a precise definition. Perhaps the most helpful starting point is the actual content of the responses of the fifteen-year-old girls. This is what they write:

WHEN A GIRL IS WITH HER PARENTS she is not herself. They think they know her but they don't.

WHEN A GIRL IS WITH HER PARENTS she becomes like them and cannot find her own identity.

WHEN A GIRL IS WITH HER PARENTS she has to behave differently.

WHEN A GIRL IS WITH HER PARENTS there are many thoughts which she feels she cannot share with them.

WHEN A GIRL IS WITH HER PARENTS she is not often her real self.

Thus it can be seen that where the girls' Negative themes are concerned one should not be thinking primarily in terms of a direct clash or conflict. Boys, expressing 'Frustration' themes, indicate that restriction, confinement and the imposition of rules and regulations are major features of their relationship with their parents, and therefore major causes of the antagonism which they feel. For girls, on the other hand, a much subtler issue of identity appears to overshadow their parental relationships, and while there are obviously Negative feelings, these centre not so much around a direct conflict as around the difficulty of being oneself. These findings, of course, fit closely with the different patterns of emotional autonomy for boys and girls described both by Kagan and Moss (1962) and by Douvan and Adelson (1966). The present evidence, however, makes it possible to go further and to look directly at the nature of the conflict as it is seen by the adolescent himself.

The graphs, and in fact all the results so far, have indicated the developmental nature of parental relationships. However there is a very real difference between the quantitative data and the immediacy of the personal feelings contained in some of the stories. Thus an attempt has been made to select a few of these for two main reasons; first, to illustrate the developmental sequence from an individual rather than a statistical point of view, and second, to carry the discussion of the meaning of conflict further by allowing those most directly concerned to speak for themselves.

The first two stories exemplify eleven-year-old responses to the family situation. In the first it is worth noting the unquestioning acceptance of parental authority, and in the second the remarkable way in which the idea of independence forces itself into consciousness, all the while being strenuously denied.

PICTURE 3.   ELEVEN-YEAR-OLD BOY

Two people are having a meal and they have an argument about their son and then their son comes in the room and finds that they have been arguing and he wonders what he has done wrong. In the end his parents tell him and he apologizes.

PICTURE 10.   ELEVEN-YEAR-OLD GIRL

This boy is looking out of a window at night. He sees the trees the flowers and all these sort of things as you would see any night. But to him its different. Because he sees it in a different way to any other person. He sees it as its all gods and god made it. He also is wondering whether to run away and leave his parents but then he feels he can't so he closes the window, has one more look out into the open and goes to bed with this feeling. In the morning his feeling has gone and he just carried on normally.

Both the thirteen-year-olds selected illustrate considerable movement, yet both illustrate in different ways the distance they have yet to go. The first still sees the likelihood of independence as so remote that the story is a dream, and even in the dream there is the necessity to keep open the option of returning without his parents knowing. In the second the restraints are perceived as external, and the description of a harsh and unsupportive world (often a major reason for fearing independence) could hardly be bettered.

PICTURE 10.   THIRTEEN-YEAR-OLD GIRL

It is a farm. It's night and John feels he's had enough and decided to run away. He opens the window in a dream then packs a few odds and ends and belongings, not forgetting his teddy although he's past 10 and jumps down into the hay below. He isn't sure of himself that's why he left the window open so he could easily get back into the house by means of a rope before his parents awoke.

PICTURE 10.   THIRTEEN-YEAR-OLD BOY
Mark thrusts open the window and instantly the cold air beats into his face, cutting across his cheeks in a cruel way. He winces and holds his right hand before his face in an attempt at protecting it from the wind, while he supports himself with his left. The clouds cover the sky making an otherwise gloomy day even worse. Mark sees his chance hasn't come yet and closes the window carefully, without a sound.

By the age of fifteen the conflict is out in the open. In fact one of the most striking things about this developmental pattern is the degree of change between thirteen and fifteen. Here there is no longer any notion that adults can be right, although there is, on the part of the girl, an acute awareness of the possible effects of behaviour upon other people. For the boy it is very much more a question of direct conflict, with little awareness or concern for feelings, just as was illustrated earlier by the 'Frustration' themes on sentence 13.

PICTURE 5.   FIFTEEN-YEAR-OLD GIRL
The little boy stood by the door, waiting for the half-chance to run out. His mother stood by it too, just in case he did. Confliction! What an appropriate word thought the mother. She had just argued with him again. She loved him so much, but just found it hard to show it. Whenever she had tried to lavish her meaningful affection on him, it always worked out wrong. So they both stood there, her striving to hang on and him striving to run off. She looked at his pitiful, tear-stained face, 'Okay, you can go' she cried. He ran out of the door and she sat down, quietly sobbing.

PICTURE 3.   FIFTEEN-YEAR-OLD BOY
The picture concerns an argument at dinner time. The son of College age, has gone home from the University to visit his parents to tell them of his plans. He wants to leave

the University and join a flower-children commune in
Birmingham. His parents object, as they want him to get
a nice job, and find a nice wife, and have nice children and
live in a nice neighbourhood. At this time a drastic falling-
out occurs, as the son gets up from the table and starts
making his point, pounding the mantlepiece to emphasize
his words.

One story of a sixteen-year-old has also been included because
it illustrates a combination which is not uncommon at this age:
a combination of independence and despair, the compulsion to
escape while knowing that the end will be disastrous.

PICTURE 10.   SIXTEEN-YEAR-OLD GIRL
He is mixed up and a Ward of Court for fighting a policeman. His father hates him and his mother can't help him
by her mute love. He's got to get out before he suffocates
with the hate overflowing in him. He's ready to risk his
life to jump out of the window to freedom whether in
death or life. He looks back once and tries to stop himself falling but loses his balance and crashes down. He
breaks his neck but he's away from hate—broken away
from life and its discomfort and prejudices and its turmoil.

By the time the adolescent is seventeen or eighteen the issues
have become very much more complex. The folowing stories
have been selected to illustrate three very common themes:
idealism, violence on the part of the boys, and emotional sensitivity on the part of the girls.

PICTURE 6.   EIGHTEEN-YEAR-OLD BOY
Two Christians are talking to a member of a very Christian
household, trying to persuade him that the Christian way
of life is the way of life for him as well. But there is an
overwhelming gap that cannot be bridged unless done so
from his side. The two are kind and considerate just like
his father and mother but they are really so far away and
he has done so many things that they, and his parents, tell
him that are wrong, how can he possibly join them? But

eventually something which he can't really describe bridges the gap for him.

PICTURE 5.   SEVENTEEN-YEAR-OLD BOY
The two people are a son and his father. The man is just about to brutally punish the boy because he's had a rough day at work, his sex life is ruined because he thinks he's impotent, and anyway the boy was making a terrible noise. It will be the usual result. The father will work out his troubles on the boy's back and receive some sadistic satisfaction while the boy will notch up one more cut of hate on the gun of his body against his father which one day will shoot the man a crippling blow when the son leaves home.

PICTURE 3.   SEVENTEEN-YEAR-OLD GIRL
There is an air of pending disaster in the picture. The two figures seated seem exceedingly comfortable and are obviously not young. The man standing, younger than the two people, leans, and seems on the point of telling the people, his parents probably, something very important. He seems to be working to sum up all his courage to utter the words! and when he finds them the father will say nothing, just look, and the mother will cry and be very sad. The son will become angry as a defence against the hurt he has caused his parents, breaking up the warm peaceful atmosphere of the home.

Finally one story in which the conflict is over. The struggle is past, independence is just round the corner, and yet there are, inevitably, second thoughts and some regrets. Mourning is undoubtedly a significant aspect of much of adolescent experience, for to give up one's childhood must involve loss, and this girl manages to capture just these feelings.

PICTURE 10.   EIGHTEEN-YEAR-OLD GIRL
'Not long to go now' he thought, 'One more week in this place and then I'm off to University. This place. My home. It'll be sad going. To think I'll probably never see this road covered with Autumn leaves again. Never walk

through that park in my school uniform again. Never sit
in this bedroom doing my homework again. Funny how,
when you've achieved everything you want to, suddenly you
don't want to accept it. Don't want to leave the routine
and security of everything you've ever known—ever loved
. . . wonder what she's doing now. The sky looks dark, sad
almost. Could I stay if I had the option? Would I *really*
want to stay here in this place, doing the same thing, the
only thing I've ever known? After all, there's no sadness
here, no unknown, only security and tradition . . . I'm
off in a week . . . '

Thus the stories illustrate something of the process of maturation in parental relationship between the years of eleven and
eighteen, as well as providing important evidence with regard
to the issues discussed at the beginning of the chapter. To recapitulate, where the amount of conflict is concerned the data
show, unequivocally, that negative attitudes towards parents
are so common among certain age groups as to be almost universal. While at first sight such evidence appears to contradict
Douvan's position it is not, in fact, difficult to reconcile both
points of view. The present findings indicate that if one is thinking of direct conflict then such a phenomenon is present in boys,
particularly at seventeen, but hardly at all among girls. Thus
when Douvan and Adelson say 'the normative adolescent tends
to avoid direct conflict with his family' they are substantially
correct as long as it is remembered that their conclusions can
apply only to girls and younger boys, since it was with these groups
that their research was carried out. We have seen that it is the
older boys who experience overt conflict, while girls feel something quite different, though equally negative; for them parents
represent, at a certain age, a threat to their identity, a feeling
expressed particularly clearly in the 'Feel Different' themes.
Thus it can be seen that while conflict, defined as a direct clash,
is a distinguishing feature primarily of the older adolescent boy,
a negative attitude to parents is a feature common to all adolescents at some time in their development.
    These findings contribute also towards an answer to the
second question, that of the focus of the conflict. It will be
recalled that Douvan and Adelson (1966) showed, for girls,

differences between age groups in the issues perceived as conflictful. They described a progression from narcissistic difficulties
(e.g. clothing and lipstick) in early adolescence, to interpersonal issues (dating), and from there in late adolescence to
conflicts over ideas and values. There is nothing in the present
study to corroborate or contradict these findings, since the
concern here has been less with the specific, with the actual
rules and regulations imposed or broken, and more with the
general issues which contribute to the parental relationship.

This is well illustrated by the stories quoted above. While the
specific is different in every case, it is a striking fact that almost
every story is concerned, in one way or another, with independence. This fact becomes even more striking if the evidence from
sentence 13 is re-examined, for this both confirms and amplifies
the pre-eminence of the independent issue. Every theme expressed in response to this sentence concerns problems of independence—you are embarrassed or ashamed to be seen with
your parents because you are still not independent; you feel
different, you cannot be yourself because you are not independent; and if you are still dependent you feel restricted, confined
and frustrated. The amplification of the evidence lies in the
crucial sex difference illustrated here. Both boys and girls are
struggling for independence, but the evidence has enabled us
to see that for the two sexes this means two quite different
things. For boys independence is freedom from constraint, the
freedom in life to behave as one wishes. For girls, however,
independence represents internal freedom, the opportunity to
be oneself and to have some autonomy with respect to one's
feelings and thoughts. It is only if these distinctions are borne
in mind that some progress can be made in settling the controversies which at present surround the area of parental
relationships in adolescence.

6

Friendship and the small group

A lot of attention has been paid, both in theory and practice, to the adolescent peer group; to its structure, its values and its importance for the individual. Some of these issues will be dealt with in the following chapter. To the subject of friendship and the small group much less attention has been paid, and as a result of this there is relatively little in the literature which explores the nature of such relationships. This is unfortunate since it will be shown that the capacity for personal friendships develops, changes and is affected by developmental processes just as the capacity for other relationships is, and furthermore that intimate friendships, particularly those between two or three people, have meaning and are as important for the individual as the larger peer groups.

One series of studies which has made a contribution in this area is the work of Horrocks and his colleagues, who were concerned with the issue of the stability of friendship. In their research (Horrocks and Thompson, 1946; Thompson and Horrocks, 1947; Horrocks and Baker, 1951) they showed that friendship becomes increasingly more stable from the age of five to eighteen, with only minor fluctuations in a trend which is almost linear. Furthermore they found only minimal differences in degree of stability between boys and girls. Their method involved asking children to name their three best friends, and repeating the same question two weeks later, from which they derived a measure of 'friendship fluctuation' based on the number of changes made during the two-week period. Horrocks makes clear that there was considerable fluctuation even at seventeen and eighteen, in spite of the steadily increasing stability with age. He explains this by arguing that most adolescents will have more than three good friends, and thus to a certain extent chance factors will influence which of the three are chosen on any particular day. In addition Gold and Douvan (1966), in an important review, are critical of the method used, arguing that a two-week time span is narrowly limited and gives very little information about real stability. It seems that in these points a number of issues are being confused. Stability over a short time span is just as interesting as that over a longer time span, though it may not be the same type of stability, and there can be no doubt that the findings of increasing stability with age and of no sex differences in this respect are important, though admittedly in need of further investigation.

Apart from the work of Horrocks and his colleagues, Douvan and Adelson (1966) probably provide the most thorough analysis of adolescent friendship in the literature, though, as has been noted, their evidence primarily concerns girls. As in other sections of their book they divide adolescence into three phases —early, middle and late adolescence—and describe the predominant pattern during each of these phases. In the early stage (eleven, twelve and thirteen years) friendship appears to 'centre on the activity rather than on the interaction itself'. Friends are people with whom things can be done but there is as yet no notion of depth or mutuality, or even of much feeling in the friendship relationship. In middle adolescence (fourteen, fifteen and sixteen) the stress is almost entirely on security. What is needed in a friend at this stage is that she should be loyal and trustworthy—someone who will not betray you behind your back. Douvan and Adelson reasonably ask the question 'Why such an emphasis on loyalty?'. Their answer is twofold. First, that the girl is seeking in the other some response to or mirroring of herself, that she is in need of someone who is going through the same problems at the same time. In some senses it could be argued that the middle adolescent girl is dealing with her problems by identification, and therefore the friend who leaves her leaves her to cope with her impulses on her own. The authors explain it by saying that 'with so much invested in the friendship, it is no wonder that the girl is so dependent on it' (1966, p. 189).

Second, Douvan and Adelson point out that middle adolescence is the time when girls first begin to date. Therefore the friend is needed as a source of guidance and support, as a person with whom she can share confidences, and as someone who will not abandon her in favour of boys. Finally, in late adolescence friendship, according to Douvan and Adelson, is a more relaxed, mutual experience. 'Needing friendship less, they are less haunted by fears of being abandoned and betrayed' (1966, p. 192). Friendship at this stage is no longer a prop or a means of resolving conflict, so that because it is more disinterested, it can involve more tolerance and sharing.

Some of these changes are reflected in the findings set out in table 6.1. One of the questions asked in Douvan and Adelson's research was 'What are the most important things a friendship should give?' and both the increased need for security in middle adolescence and the greater degree of mutuality in late adolescence are shown clearly in these figures.

Table 6.1 *Answers to question: 'What are the most important things a friendship should give?'*

	Under 14	14–16	17–18
	%	%	%
Mutuality; intimate confiding	9	18	28
Security; friend loyal trustworthy	31	52	44
Shared interest	19	16	22

It will be recalled that Douvan and Adelson did also have some data for boys in the fourteen- to sixteen-year age range, and their tentative conclusions are worth mentioning even though the evidence is not developmental in nature. They found that in general friendship for boys in middle adolescence is important as a source of companionship but as little more. There was no evidence of the stress on security and loyalty that features so prominently among the girls, and there appeared to be little notion of obligation or responsibility in this type of relationship. In short Douvan and Adelson argue that boys in the fourteen- to sixteen-year age range view friendship very much as eleven- or twelve-year-old girls do.

Another study referred to in a previous chapter, that of Powell (1955), also has some interesting evidence on the developmental nature of friendship which in some respects corroborates that of Douvan and Adelson. Powell, using the method already described involving a word association technique, showed clear age differences with respect to conflict and anxiety over friendship, the highest levels of conflict being at fifteen for boys and sixteen and seventeen for girls. Perhaps even more importantly he also showed the degree of conflict to be very significantly greater for girls than for boys at thirteen, fourteen, sixteen and seventeen.

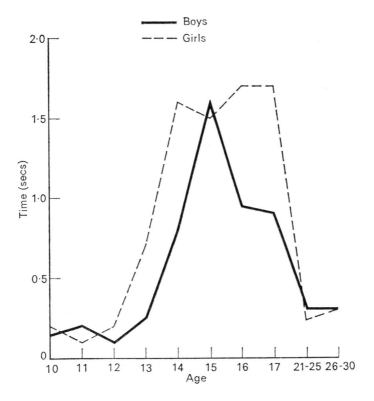

Figure 6.1 *Mean differences in reaction times between neutral and 'friendship' words on a word association test (after Powell, 1955)*

It is of interest to note the similarity between this trend and that concerned with heterosexual relationships. The two are almost identical, indicating that friendship with same sex peers during adolescence is very closely associated with attitudes and feelings regarding heterosexual relationships, and providing an important link between Powell's findings and Douvan and Adelson's discussion of the need for security in friendship in middle adolescence.

Finally Willmott's (1966) study of adolescent boys in East London provides some evidence regarding the actual time spent with friends for this group of teenagers. Table 6.2 sets out his findings.

Table 6.2 *Age and time spent with friends*

	14–15	*16–18*	*19–20*
	%	%	%
Mostly with friends in spare time	57	44	32
Sometimes with friends	28	38	42
Never with friends	15	18	26

This evidence provides a good illustration of the change in the importance of friendship during the adolescent period, showing that the fourteen- to fifteen-year group spend more time with friends than do the other age groups.

In sum these studies provide only limited evidence, and can hardly be said to combine into a broad and coherent picture of the role of friendship in adolescence. Perhaps the most consistent finding is the one indicating that fifteen years of age is a crucial period for friendship, an age at which a considerable proportion of time is spent with friends, and yet a time also when insecurity and anxiety are at their height. In looking for explanations of this phenomenon, Douvan and Adelson (1966) provide some important clues, though it may be necessary to explore further than they have done for a satisfactory solution. For example they pay little attention to the problems of rivalry and competition among friends in middle adolescence, possibly an important factor in the insecurity which is experienced. Apart from this, however, there is no consistent evidence regarding sex differences, since Powell and Douvan and Adelson show a greater degree of insecurity among girls, while Horrocks and others suggest that there are no differences between the sexes in stability of friendship. In addition very little consideration has been given to the impact of friendship from the individual's point of view, and it will be possible to turn to the qualitative evidence for some help in this direction.

The evidence

The evidence to be presented relates to a friendship situation between three people, and is based on the responses to picture 3 and sentence 3 (OFTEN WHEN THREE PEOPLE ARE TO-GETHER . . .). As usual material has initially been scored in terms of Constructive (OFTEN WHEN THREE PEOPLE ARE TO-GETHER they enjoy themselves) and Negative themes (OFTEN WHEN THREE PEOPLE ARE TOGETHER they fight like cats).

The results from sentence 3 are presented in figure 6.2, where it will be seen that there is a clear difference between age groups in the expression of Negative themes. For both boys and girls the peak for the expression of these themes occurs at fifteen, and there are significant differences between the sexes at eleven, thirteen and fifteen. On the other hand there is no evidence to show any developmental change in the expression of Constructive themes.

These trends are confirmed and corroborated by the results from picture 3 (see figure 6.3), which shows an almost identical development, except that as far as sex differences are concerned, the eleven- and thirteen-year-olds are much closer to each other than they appear to be on sentence 3.

These results are in direct support of all previous evidence in showing that fifteen is a critical age for friendship. They also give a clear indication that this type of friendship situation is more difficult for girls than it is for boys, especially at fifteen years of age. Such findings raise two major questions. On the one hand one would like to know a little more about the reasons for the sex differences, and on the other hand it is important to

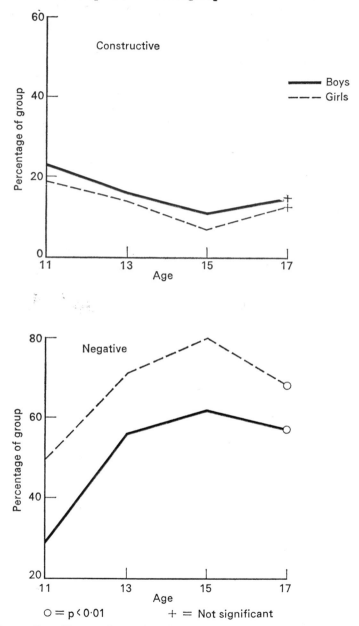

Figure 6.2 *Proportions of each age group expressing Constructive and Negative themes on sentence 3*

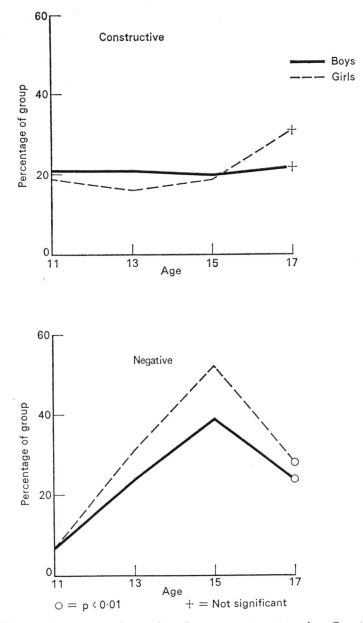

Figure 6.3 *Proportions of each age group expressing Constructive and Negative themes on picture 3*

understand why fifteen is such a critical age. What are the tensions, and why do individuals feel most threatened in this situation at this time?

One way of looking at these questions might be to give closer attention to the specific nature of the Negative themes elicited by sentence 3, and for this reason a further analysis was carried out in which a distinction was made between themes in which straightforward quarrelling or argument was mentioned (e.g. 'OFTEN WHEN THREE PEOPLE ARE TOGETHER they get cross and

Table 6.3 *Proportions of each age group expressing the two types of Negative theme on sentence 3*

Age	Rejection	Quarrel	Other	N
	%	%	%	
		Boys		
11	43	50	7	30
13	43	48	9	53
15	47	37	16	49
17	47	45	8	38
		Girls		
11	55	36	9	57
13	50	38	12	78
15	71	24	5	77
17	61	27	12	49

argue') and those where rejection or exclusion is presented as the issue (e.g. 'OFTEN WHEN THREE PEOPLE ARE TOGETHER two talk and the other one is left out'). Two particular features of the data in table 6.3 stand out. First there is a marked difference between the sexes in the overall distribution of the two types of theme. Boys express approximately equal numbers of each, while girls express a significantly greater number of Rejection themes at all ages. Second this difference is most marked at the fifteen-year level, the proportion of Rejection:Quarrel themes at this stage being roughly 3:1.

The evidence illustrates not only that rejection in a three-person situation is of more concern for girls than for boys, but that also fifteen is the age at which this anxiety is most prominent. The findings fit closely with those of Powell and of Douvan and Adelson, and it seems probable that the need for security in friendship during middle adolescence, outlined by the authors of *The Adolescent Experience,* is only one side of a coin, the other being the fear of rejection illustrated in the present material.

It is apparent that a further analysis of responses provides one clue as to the reasons behind the tensions at fifteen. A further source of information may however be the individual themes themselves. In this respect the most striking topic, apart from the actual concern with rejection already mentioned, is that of competition and jealousy which underlies a number of the girls' responses, although it is extremely interesting to note that hardly a single boy expresses such a theme. The following are some examples.

Fifteen-year-old girl: 'OFTEN WHEN THREE PEOPLE ARE TO-GETHER there is jealousy I don't know why.'

Fifteen-year-old girl: 'OFTEN WHEN THREE PEOPLE ARE TO-GETHER there is competition to speak.'

Thirteen-year-old girl: 'OFTEN WHEN THREE PEOPLE ARE TO-GETHER there are rows about who should go with who.'

Seventeen-year-old girl: 'OFTEN WHEN THREE PEOPLE ARE TO-GETHER things go wrong because of jealousies between two for the other.'

Sixteen-year-old girl: 'OFTEN WHEN THREE PEOPLE ARE TO-GETHER each one is trying to shield the other one out, to make a twosome, with one outsider.'

In spite of the fact that such themes are not expressed at all by boys, there does appear to be a masculine equivalent at fifteen. This involves a notion of power and assertiveness, the feeling that when two people are together they have a strength which is untouchable.

Fifteen-year-old boy: 'OFTEN WHEN THREE PEOPLE ARE TO-GETHER one must be omitted.'

Fifteen-year-old boy: 'OFTEN WHEN THREE PEOPLE ARE TO-
GETHER they argue and two are dominant over one.'
Sixteen-year-old boy: 'OFTEN WHEN THREE PEOPLE ARE TO-
GETHER one is left out make sure it isn't you.'
Sixteen-year-old boy: 'OFTEN WHEN THREE PEOPLE ARE TO-
GETHER two get annoyed.'

Lastly the development of one additional theme can be
traced amongst these responses. This theme has to do with a
sense of intimacy, and involves a feeling that two can be close
in a way that three cannot. Such a theme is only expressed by
the older age group, and again is almost exclusively feminine.

Fifteen-year-old girl: 'OFTEN WHEN THREE PEOPLE ARE TO-
GETHER two usually agree about something and one doesn't
and that one gets left out.'
Fifteen-year-old girl: 'OFTEN WHEN THREE PEOPLE ARE TO-
GETHER one of them feels an intruder and consequently there
is a feeling of uneasiness.'
Fifteen-year-old girl: 'OFTEN WHEN THREE PEOPLE ARE TO-
GETHER one is an odd-man-out, having less in common than
the other two.'
Sixteen-year-old girl: 'OFTEN WHEN THREE PEOPLE ARE TO-
GETHER one is in the way.'

Nothing can illustrate adolescents' experiences of this type
of peer relationship better than these individual responses.
Amongst the girls two themes predominate, both of which may
be seen to support the reasoning of Douvan and Adelson. These
themes reflect the major concerns of jealousy, competition, and
intimacy. It will be recalled that two reasons were proposed for
the stress on security and loyalty which Douvan and Adelson
found in their study. The first was the use of friendship as a
means of dealing with internal conflicts; the individual identified with and sought support from others experiencing similar
problems. Such a solution would naturally be expressed in
themes of intimacy. The second reason was the simultaneous
commencement of dating, and here the necessity for advice and
guidance was mentioned. While this specific need has not

appeared to be particularly prominent in the present study, there seems little doubt that the explanation for themes of jealousy and competition must also lie with the development of heterosexual relationships. Thus Douvan and Adelson's suggestions concerning the underlying causes of friendship tensions seem to be essentially correct, at least for girls, even though these were not taken far enough in their original discussion. For boys, however, the situation is less clear, and while it does appear that friendship has connections with feelings of power and assertiveness, there is certainly no particular evidence to explain the increased tension among boys at fifteen.

Finally some consideration needs to be given to the question of the actual impact of friendship upon individuals. In order to explore this issue it is necessary to turn to the stories, and a series has been selected to illustrate some of the ways in which friendship affects and influences adolescent development. First a large number of themes reflect the positive aspects of these sorts of relationships.

PICTURE 6. SEVENTEEN-YEAR-OLD GIRL

The people in the picture are out for a ramble in the country. They have come across a small stream which the tallest two have managed to jump across. The smallest of the three friends is just wondering how he will manage to jump across. The taller two are telling him it is very easy but he is arguing that he is a lot smaller and it isn't easy for him. In the end the other two manage to help him across the stream.

PICTURE 6. SEVENTEEN-YEAR-OLD GIRL

It is very foggy but despite this Bob wants to go to the dance tonight. He hasn't got a girl-friend so he arranged to meet two of his friends outside the dancehall. His friends are already waiting for him. Bob doesn't know his way around this area well, and with the added difficulty of the fog it is awkward to know whether you're at where you want to be at. He goes marching past the hall but his friends, thinking on the off-chance that it is him, call out to him. Now they will all be able to go into the hall and see their friends and perhaps pick up a few girls, if any

have decided to come. The three hope so, otherwise it is
5/– wasted for the ticket.

Friendship as a necessity is a second prominent theme, illustrated by the following three stories.

PICTURE 6.   FIFTEEN-YEAR-OLD GIRL
There were three friends. Originally nobody knew each
other as they were all new pupils in the first year of a
secondary school. There were 49 knew pupils altogether
and 46 of them had found their friends and had paired
off together. There was an odd number left, 3, and it
never seemed to work out. One of them always got left
out of things, you see, two is company three is a crowd.

PICTURE 6.   FIFTEEN-YEAR-OLD GIRL
There are three people here but one is separated from the
other two by a gap, a road running between them, and
they are all quietly going their own way and unaffected
by each others presence. The person alone is envious of
the others friendship but cannot bridge the distance in
between and join in. So he goes on his own way feeling
alone and unwanted but knows that he needs friendship.

PICTURE 6.   SEVENTEEN-YEAR-OLD GIRL
The gang has split up and they are going to leave me
alone again. We used to have great fun patrolling the
streets as a three, allways three together—but now they've
gone. We had a quarrel, we often had them before, but
this time they are going, and I am alone. Noone to talk
to just the air all round. I must go and find someone else,
but who? They are happy together, they can play their
schoolboy tricks together, but I have noone. I can only
watch envious.

Some stories are explicitly concerned with the influence of
friends at this stage in development, and in the following ones
issues of status are very much in evidence.

PICTURE 6.   THIRTEEN-YEAR-OLD GIRL
This is a game. The boy on the left has got to choose

whose fault it was, or who has got 'it'. He doesn't want
to be too hasty because if he is wrong he is afraid his
friends, behind him, will say he was stupid and it was
quite obvious who had it. He has to hurry to make his
decision because the other boys want a go. The other boys
are older and he thinks they will sneer at him if he gets
it wrong. He guesses and just by chance he gets it right.

PICTURE 6. SEVENTEEN-YEAR-OLD GIRL
Three boys are arguing what they are going to do that
evening. One wants to ride their bikes around the town,
but there is a heavy mist and the other two prefer somewhere else. They argue amongst themselves, they begin
shouting, they cannot agree. The mist becomes heavier
and they are getting cold. But still they argue. Eventually
one of the boys walks off. The other two watch him going.
They have argued and he has gone off on his own, to do
what he wants to do. The two boys turn around and walk
off towards the bright lights of the club down the road.
The other boy watches them, then turns around himself
and follows them down into the club.

PICTURE 3. SEVENTEEN-YEAR-OLD BOY
The people are three men perhaps brothers cousins or just
friends. The two who are sitting have tried to coax the other
into doing something which he has reservations about. He
has stood up abruptly and is trying to think it out by
himself. He has his back towards the other two because
he is trying to shut them out of his mind. He will probably agree with them in the end.

Attention has already been paid to the close link between the
role of friendship and the development of heterosexual relationships. It is interesting that remarkably few stories refer directly
to this issue, possibly because of the associated anxieties. The
stories selected are four out of a handful in the total sample.

PICTURE 6. THIRTEEN-YEAR-OLD GIRL
Ian stood back as his friend Derek picked a fight with
another boy David. They stood near to each other and

stuck their fists up. It had all started when David had
gone out with Derek's girlfriend. Derek had found out
and picked a fight with David. Ian didn't know what to
do. Should he tell Derek that he had gone with David
and he hadn't done anything . . . well not anything that
any . . .

PICTURE 6.   THIRTEEN-YEAR-OLD GIRL

Its very foggy and two blokes are walking in it. Suddenly
they saw a girl and one of the blokes said to the other
'She ain't bad, I think I'll try me luck'. So he started
chatting her up but he soon found that she didn't like
him. So as they started walking away the other one, who
was shy, said 'Your not very good at chatting up birds
let me try'. He was well away with her and got a lot off
of her.

PICTURE 6.   FIFTEEN-YEAR-OLD BOY

Chris was deeply in love with Mable. He walked down the
street thinking of her when ahead of him he saw her with
his best friend kissing and making love. This enraged Chris
and without any hesitation he knocked his friend onto the
ground. Mable began to cry, saying she wouldn't speak to
any of them anymore.

PICTURE 4.   FIFTEEN-YEAR-OLD BOY

This is a story of a boy who after going with a girl for
two years, finds that she has two-timed him. With this he
breaks it off with her. He tries to make friends but he has
little success. The first mate he makes he had a fight with.
The next he left as the mate started going with a girl. The
boy is something of a loner (a boy that likes to be left on
his own). At the time of the picture he is thinking alone
while his mates joke. The story ends with the boy going
back with the girl he first of all was going with.

Last, although it is certainly not a common feature of this
material, a few individuals do express a haunting sense of
loneliness and alienation. Since the study was anonymous it is
of course impossible to tell who these adolescents are, but they

represent just as integral a part of the sample as those who see friendship as a valuable and constructive experience.

PICTURE 6.   SIXTEEN-YEAR-OLD GIRL
This suggests to me my friends and I. We are grouped together in a certain way, and split up in another way. They behave as they do when they are in any other situation. I cannot and will not understand. I cannot seem to communicate with them they seem so close yet so far. In school we look the same but behave so differently. They cannot understand me and I do not care because I do not want their help. They do not like me being original because they say it shows them up. They think there is something wrong with me. I think there is I feel different I cannot understand myself. I think I will do myself some harm.

PICTURE 4.   FIFTEEN-YEAR-OLD GIRL
Lonely figure rejected by society. Has no friends but himself. The others gang together, talk and are spitefall, they are a menace. The lone boy is in the most envious position tho' by the droop of his shoulders he does not think so. The other groups are supposed to be friends however they are not real friends, they destroy fight and leave each other.

PICTURE 6.   SEVENTEEN-YEAR-OLD BOY
Have you ever been shunned by your friends. Oh yes it happens alright. You think that you're all good friends and that you'd do anything for them and they for you. You get on fine, then suddenly just a little something crops up and you realize that they weren't good friends after all. In fact you find yourself wondering why you ever went around with them. You think they stink. They high and mighty very superior. They go around telling everybody that you know that they always thought you were a bad type. Do you like friends. Do you ever get the feeling that your parents don't like you.

Friendship and small group situations thus provide experiences as significant and emotionally laden as other types of relationship which are more usually seen as central to the adolescent world. Friendship follows a developmental sequence which is manifestly connected with other developmental patterns; it is the cause of very considerable anxiety, and furthermore it is an area in which boys and girls have been shown to differ significantly. Generally speaking, girls express much greater tension where three-person situations are concerned, and it seems probable that this is primarily related to a sense of insecurity and fear of rejection with respect to those upon whom they are most dependent.

7

The large group

The focus of this chapter is the larger peer group, in contrast to the small group situation which has just been considered. Here the concern will be with group relationships which involve a number of participants, though there may well turn out to be close developmental similarities between the two types of interaction. In particular the present study has explored situations in which there is a relationship between the group and one individual; this includes both the individual who is separate from or rejected by the group, and the individual who assumes authority over the group. These two situations will be considered separately.

Rejection and autonomy

Feelings concerning rejection are of great importance in considering adolescent development, since the place of the individual *vis-à-vis* the group is an issue which, apart from its intrinsic interest, has implications both for the development of identity and for the influence of the peer group. The popular image of the adolescent often includes notions of excessive dependence upon the clique or gang, a slavish following of fad and fashion, and a tendency to be easily 'led astray' by the more powerful members of the group. The purpose here will be to re-examine this image, and especially to place it in some developmental perspective. Firstly, however, it will be necessary to look briefly at the background literature.

One relevant topic which has received considerable attention has been the structure of adolescent peer groups. An example

108   *The large group*

is the work of Dunphy (1963) who, in what has by now become a classic study, investigated the formation of adolescent groups in Sydney, Australia, by a combination of participant observation and more formal methods of psychological assessment. The study involved a large number of groups, and a distinction was drawn between cliques, having from three to nine members, and crowds in which the membership was considerably larger. Dunphy was able to delineate in broad outline the typical structural development of peer groups during adolescence, and in this he distinguished five stages.

The initial stage of adolescent group development appears to be that of the isolated unisexual clique; isolated because of the absence of any relationship with corresponding groups of the opposite sex. This first stage seems to represent the carry-over of the pre-adolescent gang into the adolescent period. Stage two sees the first movement towards heterosexuality in group structure. Unisexual cliques now participate in heterosexual interaction, though this is considered daring and is only undertaken with the support of same-sex colleagues. According to Dunphy interaction at this stage is often superficially antagonistic. It is at stage three that heterosexual cliques begin to form for the first time. At this stage the upper status members of unisexual cliques initiate individual contacts with members of the opposite sex, and first dating begins. It appears that the adolescents who do this also retain a foot in their original unisexual cliques as well, so that they possess, as it were, dual membership of two intersecting groups. This is the beginning of an extensive reorganization of social structure, and the end result is the emergence of entirely heterosexual cliques, which Dunphy considers to be stage four. Finally stage five sees the slow disintegration of the large crowd and the formation of cliques consisting entirely of couples who are engaged or 'going steady'. Dunphy comments as follows (1963, p. 241):

> Thus there is a progressive development of group structure from predominantly unisexual to heterosexual groups. In this transition the crowd—an extended heterosexual peer group—occupies a strategic position. Membership in a crowd offers opportunities for establishing a heterosexual role. The crowd is therefore the most significant group for the individual, but crowd membership is dependent upon

prior membership in a clique. In fact the crowd is basically an interrelationship of cliques, and appears to consolidate the heterosexual learning appropriate to each stage of development. The majority of clique members, therefore, possess a determinate position in an extended hierarchical arrangement of cliques and crowds, in which high status is accorded to groups most developed in heterosexual structure. The course of the individual's social development appears to be strongly influenced by his position within this structure.

Dunphy is careful to point out that he has not specified modal ages for the onset of any particular stage, in view of wide differences both between cliques and between individuals. However the model is clearly a developmental one, and provides helpful theoretical background for the consideration of the individual's relationship to the peer group.

Costanza and Shaw (1966) were also concerned with structure, and with the way in which this changes as a function of age. They used Asch's well-known paradigm to look at the effects of group pressure, asking subjects to make a decision regarding the length of a line where the illusion is given that all members of the group differ from the subject. The authors showed that susceptibility to group pressure was significantly related to age, though not in a straightforward linear fashion. Results indicated a relatively low degree of conformity in the seven to nine age range, the highest level of conformity between eleven and thirteen, and a gradual decrease in susceptibility to group pressure from then onwards. Interestingly the level of conformity at nineteen to twenty-one appeared to be approximately the same as it had been in the seven to nine age range, and it is noteworthy that this developmental pattern is identical for boys and girls.

Harvey and Rutherford (1960) were interested in a similar problem, though in their design subjects first made a decision involving a preference for one of two pictures in an art judgment test. Subjects then received a communication indicating the choice of a high status member of the group, and the study was concerned with the proportion of each age group who altered their choice in a subsequent task in line with the choice of the high status member. Subjects included boys and girls at nine, twelve, fifteen and seventeen, and the results indicated first, that status affected preference changes at twelve and seventeen, but not at nine or fifteen; and second, that girls were significantly more affected by status than boys at nine, twelve and fifteen, while boys' preferences were significantly more affected by this variable at seventeen. Unfortunately there is a major fault in the study, as the authors themselves point out. At the fifteen-year level adolescents in America will just have moved from junior to senior high school—in other words they will be with a new and largely unknown group of peers, which is not the case for any of the other age groups. Clearly this is a crucial variable, and renders the developmental findings open to some question. However if the fifteen-year-old age group is excluded from consideration the age changes are congruent with those found by Costanza and Shaw, while the sex differences are not.

Finally on the subject of conformity, mention may be made of a more recent study by Landsbaum and Willis (1971). These authors report research with two groups of subjects—thirteen- and fourteen-year-olds, and seventeen- and eighteen-year-olds —and they show that, when adolescents work in pairs, they are less likely in the older age group to conform to their partner's judgment of the length of a line when assessment of competence is artificially manipulated. These findings are, of course, in line with the results of previous studies.

Discussion of this area would not be complete without mention of a book which has become a landmark in adolescent psychology—J. S. Coleman's *The Adolescent Society* (1961). The main concern of this book is the way in which 'the adolescent system helps to shape identity', and one of the most important findings has to do with the nature and impact of the élite amongst adolescents. Coleman shows that it is athletic or sporting ability for boys and success in heterosexual relationships for girls which are directly associated with high status and membership of the élite, and that the adolescent's position in relation to this élite has a direct bearing on his self-image, his adjustment, and his general development. Coleman argues that, faced with this situation, the adolescent has a number of possible strategies open to him. He may conform, by attempting to excel, or at least play a part in those activities which confer status, he may rebel by becoming antisocial, or he may withdraw, leaving only his physical self in the school. Unfortunately, in view of the importance of these suggestions, Coleman provides relatively little developmental data. However there are some exceptions to this, and of particular interest in the present context is the finding that the ability to withdraw from the peer group increases directly with age. Those who were not in the leading crowd (established both by sociometry and by questionnaire) were asked whether they would like to be, and the proportions decrease for boys from 21 per cent at thirteen to fourteen to 12 per cent at seventeen to eighteen, and for girls from 25 per cent to 11 per cent through the same age range. Clearly such a developmental trend is in line with the decreasing susceptibility to group pressure found by previously mentioned writers.

It will be evident, therefore, that there is general agreement concerning the relation between age and independence from the peer group; that is to say that at least within the adolescent age range there is a decrease in dependence upon the group, which manifests itself in such things as decreasing conformity, increasing ability to withdraw from group situations, and a generally increasing individual autonomy. Such a finding may be expected in the present results. However, the details of this development are far from clear, and a particular concern of this chapter will be to look a little more closely at the actual nature of the conflict or tension between group and individual. While the broad relation between age and autonomy has been established, it is remarkable how little else is known about the dynamics of the interaction, and further clarification of this process is needed. In addition, once again the question of sex differences requires elucidation, and this will also be a focus in the analysis of the data.

The evidence
The evidence to be presented here relates to the place of an individual who is in some way outside or separate from the group. Two projective situations are relevant—picture 4, which is an outdoor setting showing a group of people under one arch and one individual under another, and sentence 2 (IF SOMEONE IS NOT PART OF THE GROUP . . .). As usual the responses have been scored for Constructive and Negative themes, where a

Negative response implies that to be outside the group is in some way harmful or damaging, and a Constructive theme indicates the advantages of being an individual. Some examples of Constructive responses to sentence 2 are: 'IF SOMEONE IS NOT PART OF THE GROUP he enjoys it because he is not following the sheep' and 'IF SOMEONE IS NOT PART OF THE GROUP they are much respected and admired'. Two examples of Negative themes would be: 'IF SOMEONE IS NOT PART OF THE GROUP he is looked upon as an outcast' and 'IF SOMEONE IS NOT PART OF THE GROUP he feels inferior to them.'

The results from sentence 2 are presented in figure 7.1. It will be seen that there are important differences between age groups for both Constructive and Negative themes, the former being expressed more at seventeen than at any other time, while the latter show a general decrease throughout the age range. There appear to be no sex differences in either of these trends.

Results from picture 4 (figure 7.2) provide confirmation of the age pattern for Constructive themes, and for Negative themes there is again a marked drop between fifteen and seventeen. The Negative trends, however, do not look similar because of the comparatively low number of Negative responses to picture 4 in the eleven- and thirteen-year-old age groups. Closer inspection of the actual results indicates that this is matched by a very high proportion of Neutral responses among these age groups, and it seems likely that the explanation for such differences is that it is much more possible for the younger age groups to express anxieties or fears on a structured sentence-completion test than it is to do so when producing an intellectually more demanding story response.

In general these results confirm the previous evidence of a developmental process. The fear of rejection, or the inability to stand outside the group, decreases with age while there is a concomitant, though gradual, increase in autonomy. As the adolescent gets older, particularly at the seventeen-year level, he begins to value independence from group pressures. What is of particular interest in these results, however, is the finding that there are virtually no differences between boys and girls in this respect. Although there is a slightly greater number of Negative themes from girls at seventeen on sentence 2, this difference does not reach statistical significance, and from all

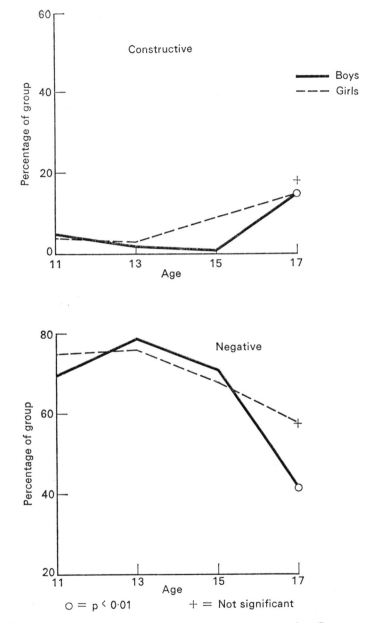

Figure 7.1 *Proportions of each age group expressing Constructive and Negative themes on sentence 2*

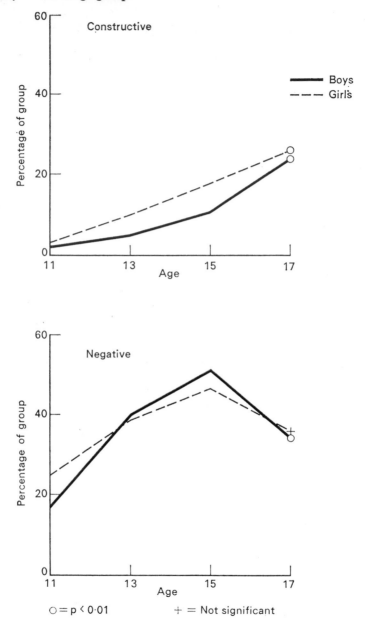

Figure 7.2 *Proportions of each age group expressing Constructive and Negative themes on picture 4*

other points of view the trends are remarkably similar. This is of especial importance in view of the contradictory nature of previous studies, and it does appear that the present data provide support for Costanza and Shaw (1966) rather than for Harvey and Rutherford (1960).

These findings having been established, it is of interest to look a little more closely at the rejection process and the feelings associated with it, since for most adolescents in the younger age groups it appears to be an emotive and anxiety-provoking situation. If it is presumed, then, that rejection or separateness is in some way a threat, the question arises as to whether the group is a threat to the individual, or the individual a threat to the group. To put it another way, is it that the teenager loses status and fears loneliness and rejection if he is not in a group, or could it be that the group itself is such an insecure network of relationships that the outsider must be ridiculed? It is possible, of course, that both these factors are operative in different situations, but it was in the hope of shedding some light on this issue that a further analysis of the Negative responses to sentence 2 was undertaken.

In order to do this, a distinction has been drawn between two types of Negative theme, one which indicates an identification with the group and a straightforward rejection of the outsider, and one which assumed an identification with the individual, indicating sympathy with or anxiety about the person who is not part of the group. Examples of themes implying a group identification are:

IF SOMEONE IS NOT PART OF THE GROUP they aren't worth knowing.

IF SOMEONE IS NOT PART OF THE GROUP they are either fat, stupid, ugly or black.

IF SOMEONE IS NOT PART OF THE GROUP you don't let them join in the fun.

IF SOMEONE IS NOT PART OF THE GROUP they get their head kicked in.

IF SOMEONE IS NOT PART OF THE GROUP we say pay a fee to join or we say get out and don't come back.

Examples of individual identification are:

IF SOMEONE IS NOT PART OF THE GROUP he feels totally uncared for and unwanted.

IF SOMEONE IS NOT PART OF THE GROUP they feel as if they
are desolate.
IF SOMEONE IS NOT PART OF THE GROUP I feel sorry for
them and help them join in.
IF SOMEONE IS NOT PART OF THE GROUP one feels afraid
one is missing something.

Table 7.1 *Proportions of each age group expressing the two
types of Negative theme on sentence 2*

Age	Group identification	Individual identification	Other	N
	%	%	%	
		Boys		
11	61	31	8	71
13	47	43	10	75
15	41	52	7	56
17	25	68	7	28
		Girls		
11	44	50	6	86
13	24	68	8	84
15	26	65	9	65
17	14	76	10	42

Differences between the sexes and between age groups are
set out in table 7.1. Generally for both boys and girls group
identification decreases throughout the age range, while individual identification shows a corresponding increase. However,
what is of even greater interest is the contrast between boys
and girls, which is graphically illustrated in figure 7.3.

There is always a higher proportion of girls, even at eleven, who
express sympathy for the individual, whereas in the eleven-
year-old group of boys the ratio is 2:1 in favour of an identification with the group. Furthermore it is not until fifteen that a
majority of boys identify with the individual rather than with
the group. Such a finding is, of course, congruent with many of
the previous results regarding sex differences which have been

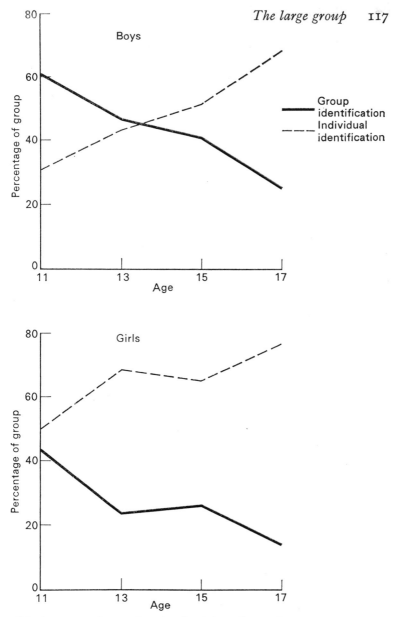

N.B. In view of the numbers involved these figures have
not been subjected to statistical analysis

Figure 7.3 *Proportions of boys and girls expressing the two
types of Negative theme on sentence 2*

discussed in this book. It also shows clearly that while approximately the same proportions of boys and girls at different ages view exclusion from the group as a negative experience this does not in any way imply that the reasons for such a perception are identical. Boys, particularly the younger ones, are closely identified with the group process. They are less caring for the individual, as would be expected from knowledge of the masculine ethos, and it may well be that precisely because of this, security and trust within the group is less certain than it is for girls.

One further means of building up a picture of the relationship between the group and the individual adolescent is to look at some of the stories, particularly those elicited by picture 4. A series of six has been selected to illustrate, in a developmental sequence, the power and influence of the group upon the individual. It will be recalled that in the previous chapter some reference was made to this issue, and one or two stories relevant to it were presented. The following elaborate much the same problem, but in a more striking manner.

PICTURE 4.   ELEVEN-YEAR-OLD BOY
The people are all friends except the one on his own. He disagrees with the other people about certain policies, he is very lonely but makes out he is happy. He is watching the others but can't agree with them, but later everything is going to turn out he realizes his mistakes and rectifies them.

PICTURE 4.   THIRTEEN-YEAR-OLD BOY
The group of schoolchildren hurry through the ruins of a church on an outing. They are all in a group except for one skinny sulking boy who tries to tag along with them but keeps getting pushed away by the others who just laugh at him and call him names. Then crying aloud the skinny boy runs into the bushes and the others follow, mocking him.

PICTURE 4.   THIRTEEN-YEAR-OLD GIRL
The group of boys are plotting a trick on the odd-one-out who's standing on his own miserably. They do not approve

of him because he is coloured. They are going to put a
pin on his chair and pretend that he was the one to write
horrid things on the blackboard about the teacher. They
will swop his neat books for those that are messy and
dirty. The boy crys and runs and goes home to bed, to
face another day of torture tomorrow.

PICTURE 4. FIFTEEN-YEAR-OLD GIRL
Five men are standing in a group on the left of the
picture. One man is standing alone at the right of the
picture. The group are discussing and will not allow him
to join in. He says he does not care and he can manage
without them, but the truth is he can't. He longs to belong
to the group and he does not know why they rebuke him
so. Because of this he becomes a loner and stays on his
own permanently. He eventually begins to hate people.

PICTURE 4. SEVENTEEN-YEAR-OLD BOY
The boys of Charlton Village were well organized into a
gang and made their headquarters in the old ruins of a
Roman villa across the meadows. So when a newcomer
came to the village, James Manton, they naturally were
suspicious of him. He begged them to let him join so they
told him to meet them at the villa the following day to
arrange 'tests' for him to take before he could join. Unfortunately he is too weak to pass them and they lounged
against the wall laughing and jeering.

PICTURE 4. SEVENTEEN-YEAR-OLD BOY
It's school when term begins, the group are boys who
have been to the school before. The only one by himself
is a new boy, he is frightened and awed by being there.
Later the next term he is with the group and it is another
who is by himself. However the boy refuses to help the
other neglectful of what he had been through previously.
The group are indifferent to the sufferings of the loner,
more interested in discussing their holiday experiences
with their friends.

While a large number of stories reflect the influence of the
peer group, there are, understandably, virtually none which

illustrate the weaknesses of the group. The following is one of
the very few.

PICTURE 4. SEVENTEEN-YEAR-OLD BOY
There are a group of figures and then further along there
is a solitary figure. The group appear to be talking together about something while the solitary figure is standing
upright and alone. The end of the story will be tragic; the
group cannot long tolerate an individualist in their
vicinity. His ideas might counter, or even shatter their
own. Therefore he must go. This does not mean necessarily
death but in whatever form it is tragic because of the lack
of individualism present in our group world. Also it could
be noted that there is much more light coming through
the gap the solitary figure is silhouetted against.

A few stories also illustrate an ability to stand outside the
group and to comment on the actual mechanics of the accept-
ance/rejection process.

PICTURE 4. FIFTEEN-YEAR-OLD BOY
The people are young boys who are at their local club.
They are talking about the plans for raising money for their
new gym. An outcast joins their group. He is shy but
intelligent. He is mocked by the others but takes no
notice. Then quite by chance he comes up with a marvellous idea for fund-raising. He is immediately accepted as
one of the group.

PICTURE 4. FIFTEEN-YEAR-OLD BOY
A boy has joined a youth club and is finding it hard to
get on with the rest of the youths. Perhaps he is shy and
so will not speak up and so the others just ignore him. He
is lonely and is looking for a friend. It would be very
easy for him to get into the wrong set if someone was to
pretend to be friendly with him. This is a typical evening
where they are all enjoying themselves and he is left out.
Unless he speaks up and joins in or someone approaches
him he will get nowhere, it is up to him.

PICTURE 4. SEVENTEEN-YEAR-OLD GIRL

Children can be very cruel, the first day at a new school, especially if it is during the term when everybody else has had a chance to make friends. The child on its own is apprehensive of entering the playground for he is afraid that the other children will mock him and hurt him. He cannot speak of these things to his parents for they would only say that he is being foolish and that he will soon make friends. So the child goes to school on his first day, he notices that all the children seem to be ruled by the dominant character noticeably physically larger than the rest. He knows to be friends with the others he will first have to make friends with him.

Finally a number of stories from the older adolescents provide individual illustrations of increasing autonomy, implying a realization that to be an individual is a more mature basis for status or self-respect than to be a member of the group.

PICTURE 4. FIFTEEN-YEAR-OLD GIRL

This scene takes place in ancient times. The person standing on his own has done something out of custom—maybe something he thought was right and just but the others didn't think so. So his 'friends' have left him and are treating him as an outcast. They are huddled together in a group, talking about him and laughing at him. But although the 'outcast' is lonely and hurt now, he will leave that group of friends and make another, and even another until he finds someone else who believes, as he does, in right and justice and will not ignore him.

PICTURE 4. SEVENTEEN-YEAR-OLD BOY

The outsider is depicted; he has not been rejected, but is rejecting the others. They are an undistinguishable mass, no individuals. He is an individual; although he used to be friends of theirs from the same background. He now has little in common with them and feels he must go his own way and leave the shelter of companionship. They do not understand but bear no malice.

PICTURE 4.   SEVENTEEN-YEAR-OLD GIRL

The cloisters of a boy's boarding school after a lesson. One group of boys with their ring-leader in their midst are plotting something which vitally concerns them but is not really of much importance. Their conversation is punctuated by schoolboy slang and cheerful familiarity which contrasts strongly with the solitude of the boy standing apart and silently watching them. He is simultaneously wishing to be one of them for their company and sense of fun but he is also rather proud of his independence and slightly despises them. He will probably always remain alone but work as a powerful influence nonetheless.

PICTURE 4.   SEVENTEEN-YEAR-OLD GIRL

The people are watching a large fire. They have all been doing something together, but by their present positions it is obvious that one is the odd man out. This is because he has had the courage to stand up for his convictions which deep down inside the others also know to be true. It will end by them coming together again but the odd man out will always remain essentially so. The others will forget that they ever believed in what he said and will continue their lives ordinarily. The odd one, however, will grow stronger as a result of his convictions.

Thus the increase in autonomy with age, as predicted from previous studies, is reflected both in the graphs and figures, as well as in the individual responses. There appear to be no sex differences where this general finding is concerned, but there is evidence to show that different motivations may be at the root of fears of rejection in early adolescence, girls seeming to be more identified with the individual and boys with the group. Such evidence has obvious links with other relationship patterns, and, in particular, close comparisons with the issues of solitude, self-image and friendship will be essential when the time comes to consider the overall course of the development of relationships in adolescence.

Authority

It is a matter of some surprise that an issue as important as the adolescent's attitudes to authority should appear, judging by the amount of attention it has received, to be of relatively little concern to psychologists. It is an issue which has enormous implications for society at large, and it is presumably at precisely this point, where adult and adolescent disagree about the nature of authority, that most conflict is likely to be generated. Irrespective of whether the authority is teacher, policeman, magistrate, or park-keeper, there seems to be a strange disinclination to examine this question too closely.

Admittedly in the last few years, under pressure from the changing university scene, there has been much concern with political activism amongst young people, and a whole literature is growing up around student culture and student personality (e.g. Bolton and Kammeyer, 1967; Keniston, 1968). However, these are problems which pertain only to a very small minority of adolescents, and they are relatively peripheral to the question at issue here, which is the development of attitudes to authority during adolescence, in particular the meaning of authority and the degree to which structure and control can be accepted at different ages. To take two examples, rare illustrations of studies pertinent to this topic are those of Newman (1966) and Horrocks and Weinberg (1970). Newman used a repertory grid to examine teenagers' concepts of authority, yet his report is entirely methodological, providing an enormous amount of information on the difficulties of analysing repertory grid material, and virtually none at all on the actual content of the adolescents' attitudes. Horrocks and Weinberg similarly were responsible for a large-scale developmental study of the needs of adolescents from twelve to twenty, but in discussing their results the authors do nothing more than state that the need to conform to external authority increases with age. Such evidence hardly contributes to a comprehensive picture of the issues involved.

Virtually the only work which is of relevance is that of Adelson and O'Neill (1966) on the growth of political ideas in adolescence. The study, which is the result of an ingenious method, is of great interest. The authors believe that most boys and girls within the adolescent age range would have some difficulty in responding to direct questions on political matters, and so within the framework of an interview they presented to their subjects the following situation (p. 295): 'Imagine that a thousand men and women, dissatisfied with the way things are going in their country, decide to purchase and move to an island in the Pacific; once there they must devise laws and modes of government.'

Having established the premise, the interview continued by offering questions on a number of hypothetical issues, by asking the adolescents to choose between different laws and different forms of government, and by posing various dilemmas in which political conflicts were expressed in concrete situations.

The sample included fifteen boys and fifteen girls of eleven, thirteen, fifteen and eighteen, and the method elicited a large amount of developmental material. Three findings of especial interest may be mentioned here. First, the authors were concerned with the adolescent's overall concept of society, and the evidence clearly shows a decline with age in the authoritarian viewpoint; the younger the adolescent the more likely he is to approve of coercion and to deem it necessary for social cohesion. Adelson and O'Neill argue, however, that this goes hand in hand with the young person's view of individuals. As they put it (p. 299): 'Younger subjects adhere to a Hobbesian view of political man. The citizenry is seen as wilful and potentially dangerous, and society therefore as rightfully, coercive and authoritarian.'

A second important area is the adolescent's concept of the purpose of laws, and here Adelson, Green and O'Neill (1969) found an interesting developmental trend which is closely related to that mentioned above. Responses were divided into those which perceived laws as restrictive only, those which saw them as beneficial only, and those which viewed them as mixed. The findings are set out in table 7.2 below, indicating unequivocally that the view of laws as coercive instruments of society decreases with age through adolescence.

Finally the evidence concerning the effects of law is of particular relevance in the present context. In the analysis of the data a distinction was made between the effects of law as External, i.e. to control behaviour; and the effects as Internal, that is to create a sense of purpose, of moral well-being and security. The results, indicating a clear developmental trend, are set out in table 7.3. It is also particularly interesting to note the remarkably high level of 'external effects' responses at thirteen, the age at which it is often assumed that the adolescent has most difficulty controlling his impulses. About these results the authors have this to say (p. 329):

> For the younger (subjects) the loss of law would produce a loss of regulation, the conduct of persons towards each other would be chaotic. Older adolescents also mention this side of the matter, but many of them go on to stress the *inner* corruption which would follow a state of lawlessness —personal confusion, anomie, and ultimately a dwindling of moral sense and capacity.

Table 7.2 *Proportions of each age group responding in different ways to the question 'What is the purpose of laws?'*

	11	13	15	18
	%	%	%	%
Restrictive	76	73	31	17
Beneficial	14	10	42	62
Mixed	10	17	27	21

Table 7.3 *Proportions of each age group expressing different responses to the question 'What would happen if there were no laws?'*

	11	13	15	18
	%	%	%	%
External effects	87	97	55	56
Internal effects	13	3	45	44

There may be some question as to whether such intensely political attitudes remain the same today as they were even ten years ago, but this is an original and important piece of work which has obvious relevance for the present research. While the two studies do not have identical concerns, Adelson and O'Neill's work is invaluable in providing a background for a developmental consideration of attitudes to authority, and also makes available a theoretical structure for the investigation of the meaning of authority in adolescence.

The evidence

The evidence in the present study concerning attitudes to authority is derived from two sources: sentence 7 (WHEN SOMEONE GIVES ORDERS TO A GROUP . . .) and picture 8, which shows steps with one figure at the top and a crowd at the bottom. Responses have again been classified as either Constructive or Negative, in this context a Constructive response being one which implies an acceptance of the concept of authority ('WHEN SOMEONE GIVES ORDERS TO A GROUP everyone thinks he will obey'), while a Negative response is one where, for whatever reason, authority is rejected ('WHEN SOMEONE GIVES ORDERS TO A GROUP we think get knotted').

The results from sentence 7 are set out in figure 7.4, from which it can be seen that there are highly significant differences between age groups for both Constructive and Negative themes. Essentially the results indicate a general decrease in the acceptance of authority with age, with a matching increase in the expression of Negative themes. It may be noted that the major difference between age groups for both boys and girls is between the eleven- and the thirteen-year-olds, indicating that the most important change in attitudes to authority occurs in early adolescence, with only gradual changes taking place from then onwards. Evidence from picture 8 (to be found in Appendix C) corroborates the developmental trend of a general increase in the expression of antagonism towards authority throughout the age range, though in response to this picture there are so few Constructive themes that in this respect no age differences are discernible.

The data raise a considerable number of issues, and in particular some consideration needs to be given both to the precise meaning of authority in this context, as well as to some of the possible reasons for the developmental trends illustrated above. First, the concept of authority in this study has deliberately been left indeterminate. In sentence 7 the individual giving orders to the group is unspecified, and in picture 8 the figure at the top of the stairs can be perceived as almost anyone imaginable. Judging from the actual responses virtually every type of

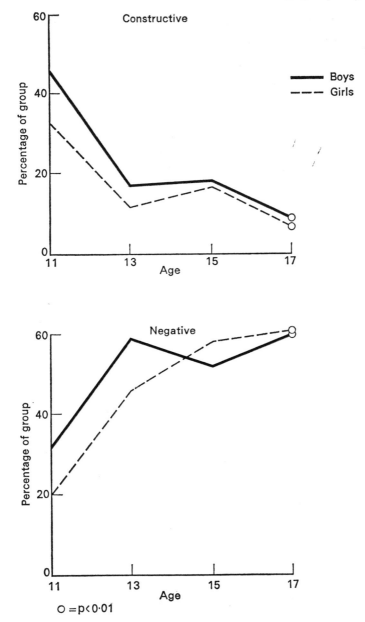

Figure 7.4 *Proportions of each age group expressing Constructive and Negative themes on sentence 7*

authority figure has been involved, ranging from older teenagers to teachers, priests, political figures, abominable snowmen, policemen and football referees. In many senses this is similar to the situation obtained in Adelson and O'Neill's research where, for example, the general concept of 'laws' has been used as the stimulus rather than anything more concrete. Experience, however, shows that adolescents respond in various ways to different authority figures, and this needs to be borne in mind for further research in this area. For the present, though, it should be noted that the results refer to a general concept of authority rather than to any specific figures or situations.

With regard to the second question a further analysis of sentence 7 proved unproductive. However, picture 8 supplied a wealth of fascinating material, and within this were to be discovered important hints concerning the next stage of investigation. It soon became apparent that many of the stories centred around a conflict between the crowd and authority, but there were also a significant number which indicated a feeling of fear or terror of whoever was at the top of the steps. In view of this a distinction was drawn between those stories reflecting Conflict, and those reflecting Fear. The following story, in response to picture 8, exemplifies the Conflict theme.

> In the foreground are a crowd of demonstrators who are yelling abuse at the man on the platform. He is an unpopular politician. He stands aloof, guarded by his strongarm men. He curses the demonstrators as unruly rabble. He yells in a tremendous voice down the microphone in an attempt to drown his yelling opponents. Eventually he gives up when the crowd become ugly and start to throw things at him.

The following story illustrates the theme of Fear:

> A feeling of terror and panic. Some unknown, hitherto unexperienced being descending the steps towards a crowd of people. They turn and try to flee pushing and jostling in their fear, but the survival of the fittest is in order. Many people are trampled underfoot, the steps become a stream of flowing blood and people. A few have escaped the being still advances.

The result of this analysis is shown in table 7.4. It can be seen that on the whole boys express very few Fear themes, nor do there appear to be any striking changes with age in the ratio of Fear:Conflict themes in their responses. Girls on the other hand express quite a substantial number of Fear themes, and furthermore this expression does show some limited relation to age. The proportion of themes expressed increases through the age span, and by seventeen more Fear than Conflict themes are being elicited from girls. This is an important distinction and can be seen to be in line with many other differences between boys and girls already discussed.

Table 7.4 *The proportions of each age group expressing two types of Negative theme on picture 8*

Age	Conflict	Fear	Other	N
	%	%	%	
		Boys		
11	82	9	9	33
13	70	26	4	43
15	80	6	14	32
17	75	22	3	37
		Girls		
11	60	33	7	40
13	67	23	10	47
15	59	37	4	46
17	40	52	8	44

For boys, the relationship to authority involves confrontation. Authority, whether it be in the form of parents or policemen, represents a challenge, and it is expected that an attempt will be made to stand up to it. For girls, on the other hand, the conflict is very much less direct, in fact quite often there is no conflict at all. Authority, presumably representing force or power, is perceived as something frightening or terrifying, something to flee from, something that is destructive yet unknown and 'unexperienced', as one individual expressed it. In some senses it is precisely this unknown quality which makes the difference between boys and girls. It is apparent that boys do have an idea of who or what it is they have to confront, and so they perceive their relationship with authority in terms of a direct conflict. For some reason girls do not have available to them a straightforward authority structure. They seem to be less sure exactly where the boundaries lie, and perhaps it is for this reason that authority, when it appears, is more difficult to grapple with, being seen therefore as both frightening and unknown.

There is little doubt that this sex difference is a crucial factor in the understanding of the development of adolescent relationships, for it elucidates the two major forms in which the authority problem presents itself to young people, as well as revealing possible channels through which such problems may be resolved. None the less the picture is far from complete and, as in previous chapters, some of the individual stories will help to provide depth and to underline the reality of the authority issue for the adolescent. The following four stories are a random selection from the older age groups, illustrating in different ways the negative components of the authority concept.

PICTURE 8.   SEVENTEEN-YEAR-OLD BOY

There are a group of people and one advancing from above. The group are sitting at the bottom of the steps—the steps of life—and the shadow is of one who will help these people to throw off their oppressors and rise—for his own benefit. The picture is one of Fascism—at the bottom are the German people—discontented, revengeful, young, coming from above is Hitler with all his masterful eloquence and propaganda. He is coming to make these people fight, and die for HIM, not for themselves. He fills them with dreams and hopes so easy to grab hold of if you are discontented, and then he pushes them gently over the edge of the abyss into war.

PICTURE 8.   SEVENTEEN-YEAR-OLD GIRL

A political orator is talking to the crowd—again confrontation between one and many. The crowd are angry but they are also confused and have no spokesman and

no common voice. He has the power born of a dictator
since he voices one opinion alone and is conscious that he
can sway the people to his will by deceptive eloquence.
Mark Antony perhaps in Shakespeare's Julius Caesar. He
hates and despises the crowd because he feels superior and
they, conscious of this intangible superiority, rail against
it but cannot somehow break the gap between him and
them because he holds them by his power and their own
sense of inferiority.

PICTURE 8.   FIFTEEN-YEAR-OLD GIRL
This is a picture of some steps outside a building. At the
bottom of the steps is a gang of people and at the top is
a man. The people at the bottom of the steps are rioting
because of the rent increase and at the top of the steps
is Mister Cutler telling them that they ought to pay the
rise. The crowd are jeering, police try to hold them back
but its no use the crowd storm through and run up the
stairs screaming 'not a penny on the rent'. Mister Cutler
is dragged into the building and the door is slammed on
the anguished faces.

PICTURE 8.   FIFTEEN-YEAR-OLD GIRL
These are people who are afraid of something which is
above them. They have no idea who or what it is and
some people have doubts as to whether there really is
such a thing or whether they are just all imagining something so much that it becomes real to them. The thing in
the top left corner is the thing, and the people underneath
are trying to escape from it but all the time they feel that
they just cannot get away from a thing which probably
does not really exist.

The expression of fear and the unknown is particularly well
expressed in the last of these. Not all adolescents however view
authority as a bad thing, and a sense of idealization is power-
fully conveyed in the following selection.

PICTURE 8.   FIFTEEN-YEAR-OLD BOY
There is one important person and a crowd. The crowd

have just seen the prime minister come out of a very
important building after having talks with other leaders.
The prime ministers staff tell the crowd to go back and
let the leader pass, but the crowd is angry about one of
their policies. Unexpectedly the prime minister comes
forward and speaks to the crowd. Everyone is astonished.
The crowd respond, grow quiet and listen to the prime
minister. The prime minister is very loyal and eloquent
and he soon moves the crowd to sympathy instead of
anger.

PICTURE 8.   SEVENTEEN-YEAR-OLD GIRL
The people at the bottom of the stairs are a mob who are
extremely angry but for some reason they dare not go
up any further. The shadow of the figure coming down to
them is of someone with almost Saint-like qualities who
is not afraid of them having an almost hypnotic power
over them. He will succeed in calming the people and they
will not cause trouble for a long time again.

PICTURE 8.   SEVENTEEN-YEAR-OLD BOY
The people at the bottom of the picture are waiting at the
bottom of a long flight of stairs. They are waiting for the
person whose shadow appears at the top of the picture,
who is descending the stairs. This person is their hero
and they are mad with jubilation at being able to see him
in person. He will come down to them and they will paw
at him and ask him for autographs after which he will
ascend the stairs.

Some of the stories are not so straightforward, and a number
reflect a mixture of awe and mockery which is hard to describe
but is well illustrated in the following three responses.

PICTURE 8.   FIFTEEN-YEAR-OLD GIRL
The new king has just been crowned, he is standing at
the top of the steps of his palace surrounded by body
guards—he has to be, he could easily be shot by the mass
of the people at the bottom of the steps. All of them are

'worshipping' their new king, but anyone of them could be a potential assassin. Many people disagree with the choice of king. The new king is a good king, he wasn't assassinated at his coronation. He was shot the following day.

PICTURE 8. SEVENTEEN-YEAR-OLD GIRL
The President remained calm and held his position at the top of the steps whilst the crowds below mocked and laughed at him. Here he was the man who had ruined their country, because he had not the courage of his convictions, and now he was trying to look so courageous in the face of his downfall, that to the people it appeared as one big joke.

PICTURE 8. SEVENTEEN-YEAR-OLD BOY
This is a prehistoric gathering of sun worshippers. The high priest of the cult, whose shadow can be seen at the top is performing some sort of rite to coincide with the appearance of the sun. The way this is done gives the effect that the sun's rising is the direct result of what he has done—hence the surprise amongst the spectators.

Finally, one or two do begin to cross the gap between follower and leader. A few express the realization that they too will have to assume the authority in due course, and that it will be a strange and possibly frightening experience. This story is a good example:

PICTURE 8. SIXTEEN-YEAR-OLD GIRL
He comes, haltingly down the steps, warily eyeing the crowd at the bottom.
'I hate crowds', he thought. Nearer and nearer he got to them. He imagined himself struggling to get through, breathless, afraid of being trampled underfoot, almost . . .
He reaches the bottom. The crowd parts, respectfully, allowing him an ample pathway.
'Of course!' he thought, 'I must remember that I'm their new leader, not just one of them anymore'. He smiled at the people, who up until now, had been his equals.

The issue of authority is a salient feature of every relationship, but it is particularly critical for the adolescent, especially with respect to adults, because of the pre-eminence of the movement towards autonomy. The present findings have shown that, as a general rule, negative attitudes towards authority figures increase with age during adolescence, with a particularly marked difference between the eleven- and the thirteen-year-old age group. However the results have also indicated an important sex difference, in that boys' feelings appear to involve a greater degree of outright conflict while those of girls are strongly associated with a sense of fear. Apart from this last point, on which they provided no evidence, such findings complement the work of Adelson and O'Neill. These authors showed that among younger adolescents there exists a belief that coercive laws are necessary for society, and that the purpose of laws in general should be to restrict and to control individuals. This is corroborated by the present findings that in early adolescence young people are more likely to accept and be sympathetic to authority. Adelson and O'Neill see their findings as being connected with difficulties in impulse control at the time of puberty, a point of view which fits well with explanations which have been proposed in the present study. In fact the specific sex differences illustrated above, as well as the move towards independence and away from the acceptance of authority, symbolize the more general concept of the adolescent process which has been developed in this book.

8

A focal model of adolescent development

In previous chapters individual relationships have been investigated, and with this information it will now be possible to take
a broader look, and to explore some of the ways in which the
development of these different areas is linked together. Each
relationship has represented another facet of the adolescent's
world, and the time has come both to consider the material in
its entirety, and to examine theories of adolescent development
in the light of the present findings.

As has been mentioned before, one important element of any
realistic approach to a developmental period is a holistic orientation. While it may be essential to break down the field into
discrete units for the purpose of analysis, the process will be
incomplete until the whole is brought back into focus. In the
present context it seems highly probable that the course of each
individual relationship during adolescence will have some bearing upon others, and only by considering all relationships
together will a coherent picture emerge. The intention up to
this point has been to look, for example, at the peak age for
difficulties with parents, or the time at which solitude is most
likely to be seen as a constructive experience. Now the interaction between these processes needs to be examined.

Theories of adolescence, some of which have been reviewed
earlier, imply different views of the pattern of development.
For example the theory which has here been designated as the
'storm and stress' approach implies that adolescence is a time
of generalized crisis, and does not go further than to provide an
image of a series of difficulties in relationships, all likely to be
occurring at approximately the same time. Role theory, on the

other hand, takes the view that each relationship will look
different to the various participants, and that each individual
will play a series of different roles, the role being partly dependent upon the person with whom the individual is interacting.
However there are no explicit developmental assumptions
underlying this approach, and so there is no prediction concerning the expected time course of events. It is undoubtedly
stage theory which has the most to say about the developmental
process, for here there is the obvious implication that each age
will be represented by a distinctive pattern of relationships.
One limitation, however, is that within this approach little
attention has been paid to the question of links between elements
in different stages.

A moment's thought will, of course, indicate that relationships cannot be divorced from each other—friendship and
heterosexual relationships, parents and other authority figures,
solitude and friendship—all these are likely to influence one
another, and one of the unique opportunities provided by this
study has been the chance to look at precisely these interrela-
tionships. In order to do this it will be worthwhile to set out in
tabular form the ages at which individual issues appear to be
most prominent. Since the material has been analysed in terms
of Constructive and Negative themes it is possible to indicate
the peak ages for the expression of these two types of attitude
for each relationship. The peak age is simply the point at which,
in comparison with other age groups, the greatest proportion
of the group expresses a particular theme. Boys and girls have
been considered separately in tables 8.1. and 8.2. (The actual
data upon which the tables are based are to be found in Appendix C.)

The impact of these tables lies in several areas. First, they
appear to be surprisingly obvious, in the sense that they are
exactly what might have been expected. In addition, they
present a picture of adolescence which is meaningful and
coherent; and last, one cannot help but be struck by the excep-
tional similarity between boys and girls—except for one item
the two tables are identical. Essentially the data illustrate three
patterns; the first is one in which parents and authority are
perceived, relatively speaking, as a positive force, while being
alone and heterosexual relationships represent areas of conflict.

Table 8.1 *The peak ages for boys in the expression of Constructive and Negative themes to the various relationships studied*

Age	Constructive themes	Negative themes
11	Parental relationships Authority in large group	Solitude Heterosexual relationships
13		
15	Heterosexual relationships	Friendship in small group Rejection from large group
17	Solitude Rejection from large group	Internal conflict over future identity Parental relationships Authority in large group

Table 8.2 *The peak ages for girls in the expression of Constructive and Negative themes to the various relationships studied*

Age	Constructive themes	Negative themes
11	Parental relationships Authority in large group	Solitude Heterosexual relationships
13		
15	Heterosexual relationships	Parental relationships Friendship in small group Rejection from large group
17	Solitude Rejection from large group	Internal conflict over future identity Authority in large group

The second pattern is one which primarily involves peers; heterosexual relationships are highly valued, friendship in a small group and rejection from the large group, as well as parental relationships for girls, are issues associated with a considerable degree of anxiety. In this part of the picture the interrelation between the constructive and negative elements is particularly clear. Finally a pattern can be seen in which the major difficulties revolve around future identity, authority and parental relationships for boys. This is matched by an increasing ability to value both independence from the pressures of the large group, and the opportunity of being on one's own.

Thus there seem to be three clearly delineated patterns, each containing positive and negative factors, which come into prominence at different ages. Each has a balance of its own, and the separate elements in each combination add up to a coherent whole. The strange blank at the thirteen-year age level requires some explanation. Although quite obviously as much is happening at this stage as at any other time during adolescent development, it appears from this evidence to be a transitional age at which none of the themes or issues considered here are of peak concern or attain particular prominence.

The process of describing age patterns imposes a special perspective on the evidence, for inspection involves looking across the tables, and the perspective is thus similar to that which would be taken in a stage theory approach. The findings can, however, be viewed lengthways; that is, each side of the picture can be considered separately. Taking the left-hand side first, if Constructive themes are considered to indicate relationships which at the time are most valued and most needed, then a sequence can be seen which starts with parents and authority figures, shifts to heterosexual relationships, and concludes with independence and individualization. Such a maturational process is entirely congruent with what is already known about adolescence. The early stress on structure and authority is consistent with the psychoanalytic view of puberty as a time of marked anxiety concerning impulse control, and also fits well with Adelson and O'Neill's findings illustrating the young adolescent's fears of loss of control in a political and social context. Next the acceleration of the psychological move away from home and parents, and the accompanying search for alternative love objects leads not surprisingly to the idealization of hetero-sexual relationships. Last, as might be expected in a process that is essentially maturational, the third stage involves the resolution of the dependency conflict, and the establishment of the young person as an autonomous individual in his own right.

On the right-hand side of the chart are to be found the issues which are most likely to be perceived as areas of conflict or tension. Here the sequence begins with solitude and hetero-sexual relationships, is followed by insecurity in the peer group, and ends with future identity and authority. In addition parents appear in the middle of the sequence for girls, and in the final stage for boys. Once again such a course of events is corrobo-rated by what is already known. Heterosexuality is precisely the issue which would be expected to give rise to anxiety during puberty, and fears of solitude fit well with the problems of impulse control mentioned above. Friendship and peer group tensions are hardly surprising where dependence on peers is greatest, and to this must be added the jealousies and anxieties revolving around heterosexual involvements. For girls this stage is also linked with parental conflicts, which suggests that the 'Feel Different' issue—the major source of conflict with parents—is closely connected with the development of female sex-role identity. Lastly the establishment of adult indepen-dence must be intrinsically linked with the issue of future identity, as well as involving a final struggle with authority, a struggle which for boys also includes the parental relationship.

It may be felt that too little has been made of the one sex difference in these results. It does not appear to be a very major difference, simply that the peak time for conflict with parents comes earlier for girls than it does for boys. It would be possible to explain this as a function of the generally earlier development of girls. They reach puberty earlier, they are sexually mature at an earlier age, and therefore the course of parental relationships is correspondingly advanced. However the striking similarity between boys and girls in all other relationship patterns tends to weaken this explanation. A more likely solution to the prob-lem, it seems, is that the parental relationship is the one which is most different in kind for the two sexes, and precisely because of this conflicts reach their peak at different ages. However,

this question is really part of a much more general consideration of sex differences, to which it is now possible to turn.

In their book *The Adolescent Experience* Douvan and Adelson
lay considerable stress on the importance of sex differences in
adolescent development. In fact this appeared to be one of the
major findings of their research, and they argue cogently for
the necessity of viewing the adolescence of boys and girls as
two quite separate processes. In summarizing their results, and
in discussing what they call 'the adolescent crisis' they write
(1966, p. 350): 'there is not one adolescent crisis, but two major
and clearly distinctive ones—the masculine and the feminine'.
Since quite surprising similarities between the sexes have
already been noted in the present evidence, it is clearly essential
to look more closely at this whole question. Before this is done,
it is important to recall the design of Douvan and Adelson's
research, for although they included girls throughout the adolescent age range, only boys between fourteen and sixteen took
part in the study. Thus any sex differences they found are
pertinent only to the middle adolescent period, precisely the
time at which, as shown in the present findings, boys and girls
appear to differ with regard to parental relationships.

So far in this chapter a relatively general overview of the
results has been considered, reflecting the broad temporal
sequence of events. In more specific terms the actual data, that
is the proportions of groups expressing Constructive and Negative themes, illustrate a number of quantitative differences.
These are differences which are consistent, which are statistically significant and which are corroborated both between tests
and between individual items within tests. There are four major
differences of this sort.

1. *Solitude* In this area girls consistently express a higher proportion of Constructive themes, especially in the eleven-year
age group.

2. *Heterosexual relationships* In this situation boys in the
eleven- and fifteen-year-old age groups express a higher proportion of Negative themes.

3. *Parental relationships* The quantitative data bear out the
fact that the most important sex differences occur in this area.
First, girls express a higher proportion of Constructive themes at
fifteen and seventeen, and correspondingly boys express a

greater number of Negative themes at seventeen. In addition, girls express significantly more Negative themes at the thirteen-year level.

4. *Friendship* Here girls consistently express a greater proportion of Negative themes, and this is particularly striking at eleven, thirteen and fifteen.

To recapitulate to this point, findings indicate that girls value, and are more easily able to tolerate, solitude than boys, while boys in turn find a triangular friendship situation markedly less difficult than do the girls. In addition boys are more likely to feel negatively towards the opposite sex at eleven and fifteen. Where parents are concerned girls appear to have a greater degree of difficulty in the early stages, while boys are considerably more involved in parental conflict in the older age groups. Before such findings are considered in a theoretical context, it is important to look briefly also at the sex differences occurring where further analyses of the data have been carried out. In some respects it may be argued that these differences are more telling than the ones already mentioned.

1. *Parental relationships* Negative themes expressed by boys are more likely to reflect feelings of direct frustration, while Negative themes expressed by girls indicate identity difficulties which focus upon the problem of 'feeling different' when together with parents.

2. *Friendship* Where Negative themes are concerned girls express a significantly greater proportion which indicate fears of rejection in a three-person situation.

3. *Rejection in the large group* With regard to this issue girls express more themes which imply an identification with the individual, while boys express a greater number indicating group identification.

4. *Authority* In response to this situation boys express a very high proportion of themes implying overt conflict. Girls, on the other hand, express fewer of these themes and a much greater proportion indicating fear of authority, itself often perceived as unknown and intangible.

Looking back it can be seen that three different ways of looking at boys and girls have been outlined. One can look at the overall developmental course of events; that is, the ages at which the various issues attain prominence, and here virtually no sex differences have been found. The terrain, the peaks and troughs as it were, appears to follow a remarkably similar course. However, it is also possible to look at the quantitative nature of the peaks and troughs, and here some important differences are indicated, though none are exactly dramatic. Finally, the qualitative nature of the individual issues may be considered, and in a sense it is in this material, reflecting the finer texture of the relationships, that the most interesting differences found. Before these are discussed it is important that distinctions between the three approaches are clarified.

It is of course precisely because there are different viewpoints that so much disagreement is possible where adolescent development is concerned, and this makes it especially necessary to underline the contrasts between the three perspectives. The first is temporal in nature; it illustrates, in relative terms, the interaction between time and maturation, with regard specifically to relationships in the present context. The second is concerned with degree or quantity. How much conflict is there at a particular age, and is one sex more affected than the other? The third perspective concentrates on the quality of relationships. What exactly is the nature of such and such a difficulty, and is the experience, irrespective of the numbers involved, similar for boys and girls?

Essentially this study has shown that the degree of difference between the sexes varies as a function of the particular perspective. The developmental sequence is much the same for boys and girls, the amounts of conflict differ to some extent in some areas at different ages, but most important the quality of many relationships proves to be quite different. This is not a finding which will surprise many readers, although the implications of the first two perspectives may seem unfamiliar at first sight.

Without too much distortion the study may be said to have been primarily concerned with three areas—parents, peers and identity; the three major issues, in fact, of adolescent development. Let us consider each in turn. Conflict with parents, it appears, starts earlier and ends earlier for girls. Even more significant than this, however, is the fact that the conflict revolves around different issues, which may be the major reason for the slightly differing time course. For boys the conflict is to do with independence of action, freedom of movement, true behavioural autonomy. Girls on the contrary do not indicate this to be an issue. They rarely express themes of direct conflict, but are much more frequently concerned with inner autonomy. Girls want to be able to be themselves. They feel threatened, sometimes even overwhelmed, by the influence and forcefulness of their parents, and they are clearly anxious that they will not be allowed to be the person they want to be. This is where the real conflict lies for them.

This hypothesis receives support from the evidence on attitudes to authority in the large group. It will be recalled that here girls express themes of fear, boys of direct conflict, reflecting an almost identical distinction to the one found in parental relationships. It also fits well with much of the evidence concerning more generalized sex differences. Out of the large literature on this subject two particular examples spring to mind. In the excellent longitudinal study entitled *From Birth to Maturity*, Kagan and Moss (1962) note the striking differences between boys and girls with respect to the stability over time of dependency and aggression. They show that in general terms dependency remains relatively stable for girls but not for boys from childhood to adulthood, while on the other hand aggression remains stable during development for boys but not for girls. This they explain with reference to the traditional standards for sex-appropriate behaviour, arguing that characteristics will be reinforced when they are congruent with sex-role expectations, and discouraged when they are not. In this situation dependency would be rewarded, and therefore stabilized, in girls, while aggressive behaviour would be treated similarly in boys. Such a differential pattern of adult behaviour is consistent with their results, and corresponds very well with the present findings.

In the more recent book *Males and Females* (Hutt, 1972) large numbers of studies are cited illustrating the greater degree of aggressive behaviour among males, especially among pre-school children, and the more frequent expression of affiliative behaviour in girls. Of particular interest in this work is the evidence relating biology and psychology. Hutt argues strongly against a strictly social-learning explanation, suggesting that there are constitutional as well as social-psychological factors involved here. The interpretation of adolescent relationships with parents and authority expressed in the present study is strengthened and supported by such writers as these. Boys are more aggressive and their relationships are therefore character-ized by direct confrontation; girls on the other hand are more dependent and affiliative, and these traits are reflected in the quality of their relationships with adults. This is not to say that both sexes do not experience fundamental difficulties in their relationships during adolescence, but simply that for boys and girls these difficulties are manifested in different ways.

The writings of Hutt and of Kagan and Moss are consistent also with the findings of the present study concerning peer groups. Two major sex differences have been identified here; first, rejection from a small peer group is a much greater worry for girls than it is for boys, and second, where an individual is rejected from a large group girls are more likely to identify with the individual, whereas boys express less sympathy for the individual, and are more likely to identify with the group itself. This is exactly the sort of contrast which might be expected, assuming the dissimilarities with regard to affiliation and aggres-sion. In the adolescent situation, where support from peers is especially critical, it makes sense that fears of rejection are greatest amongst the more dependent group, and furthermore that where there is an opportunity to identify either with the individual or the group the more affiliative will, with a greater capacity for empathy, select the individual. In a sense the group represents strength and power, toughness and harshness, and the boy's aggressive needs will facilitate and encourage his identification with these features of the situation.

Paradoxically identity, as it has been treated in the present study, is the area where fewest sex differences have been detected. It is true that girls are more able to tolerate and value the experience of solitude, but apart from this finding variation between the sexes has proved to be negligible. Neither group shows any particular developmental change with respect to self-image, and at no age level are there any significant differences between boys and girls. This result casts some doubt on Erik Erikson's views concerning the presence of an identity crisis in late adolescence. However, following Douvan and Adelson, a distinction has been drawn between present and future identity, and this has revealed some evidence of developmental change.

Essentially, the results show that concern over future identity increases with age, being greatest in the seventeen-year-old group, but that the pattern for boys and girls is not at all dissimilar. These findings are of considerable interest, and are amongst the many in this study which will undoubtedly repay further investigation.

Having identified a number of continuing problems, reviewed the evidence and provided tentative suggestions for the resolution of some of the issues, it is now possible to reconsider models and theories of adolescent development. Based on the results of the present study it seems reasonable to argue that adolescence is a developmental period during which, because of a unique combination of social, psychological and physiological factors, various relationships, all of which are in existence at other times, become foci of tension or conflict. This includes relationships with parents, with friends, with authority, with large groups, with small groups, and refers also to the whole issue of identity. At this time the individual, because of pressures both from within and without, experiences a greater degree of uncertainty and upheaval than at most other times in his life, and this situation is reflected to a very large extent in the pattern and quality of his relationships. However the conflicts and anxieties do not appear to cluster all together at one particular time, but rather to be spread throughout the adolescent period, each coming into focus and then disappearing into the background at different stages. In addition, of course, there are clearly very wide individual differences with respect to the temporal sequence of events.

Adolescence, therefore, is characterized by a fundamental process of reorientation in a wide range of relationships, and there is even a possibility that the individual's developmental status may be judged by his standing *vis-à-vis* this process. It has been possible, in the present study, to illustrate the striking differences between age groups in attitudes and feelings about these relationships. It has been possible to chart their developmental course, and to show the ways in which the issues provide support or create anxiety at various moments. Perhaps the most helpful and meaningful approach is to consider that the adolescent inevitably faces a series of potentially conflictful relationship situations, all of which at times create problems for him.

Each of these appears to be more prominent at one stage than at any other, though at each stage there is a significant minority who find other situations just as difficult.

With this point of view in mind it now makes sense to turn to a consideration of the three main theoretical approaches mentioned earlier, specifically stage theory, the 'storm and stress' approach, and role theory. Of the three the present study has shed least light on the last of these. This is unfortunate, but is a result more of practical constraints than of any fundamental disagreement. A recent paper which derives its impetus from role theory (Stierlin and Ravenscroft, 1972) talks of a 'transactional' model of adolescent behaviour, and it seems that this notion captures exactly the nature of the social-psychological point of view. There is no doubt that the inclusion of such a perspective would have been a great improvement in the present study, but it has just not been practically possible to give consideration to transactions, since this would have involved the investigation of the attitudes of all the relevant parents, teachers and friends. However this is not to say that the notion of interaction, particularly amongst different relationships, has not played a very significant part in the present study, nor that the actual findings bear no relevance to role theory.

Attention has been paid to the question of self-image, and an important distinction between types of identity has been carried a step further. In addition, although the exploration of relationships has been one-sided, much has been learnt of what might be expected in various interpersonal situations. For example, with respect to parental relationships it has been possible to determine the different roles to be anticipated from boys and girls, and at what ages these roles are most likely to play a part in family interaction. Similarly by looking at peer groups it has been possible to ascertain that fears of rejection are more likely to be an important feature of this situation for girls than for boys, and again the relation between this phenomenon and age has been outlined. Thus while it is true that only internal sources of motivation have been examined, such evidence is none the less pertinent to any understanding of the transactional process.

Mention has, however, also been made of one important weakness in the social-psychological approach, namely that it does not incorporate a developmental dimension. The theory is essentially concerned with the here and now, with making sense of existing networks of roles and expectations, and writers such as Rosenberg and Brim exemplify this well. If one were to illustrate visually the role theory model of adolescence it might in simplified form look something like this:

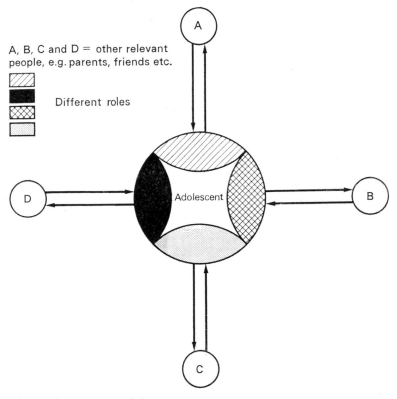

Figure 8.1 *Role model*

Perhaps in future theoretical formulations as well as in social-psychological research the model might be modified to look something like figure 8.2.

Turning to the 'storm and stress' approach, it will be recalled that a central tenet of theorists writing from this point of view is that adolescence is a time of fundamental disruption rather than of stability. The large majority of contributors to this approach have worked within the psychoanalytic framework, and their perception of adolescence has been dominated by notions of maladaptive behaviour, of pathology and of serious disturbance in relationships. Although there is no doubt that this model is more developmental in nature than role theory, there is still relatively little concern here with particular temporal predictions. Only passing references are made to a differentiation between stages, and the implication in the writings of, for example, Spiegel and Ackerman is of an undefined period of generalized disruption rather than of any specific developmental sequence.

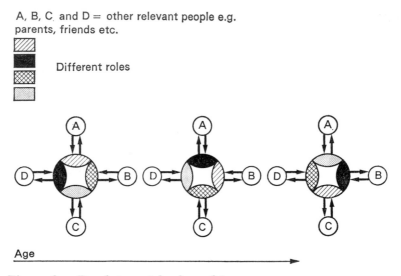

A, B, C and D = other relevant people e.g. parents, friends etc.

Different roles

Age

Figure 8.2 *Developmental role model*

It will also be recalled that there is a considerable body of evidence which contradicts 'storm and stress' theory. This stems both from a number of empirical studies which have been based on an interview technique, as well as from the social-psychological literature which illustrates a marked lack of attitude discrepancy between generations. How does the present study stand in relation to these issues?

In general terms, clear evidence has been provided which verifies the existence of a considerable degree of tension and conflict in all relationships. In particular, where parents are concerned both boys and girls experience a peak age of difficulty, although for the two sexes this differs in quality, and it is among the older groups of adolescent boys that there is the strongest evidence of direct behavioural conflict. However these findings may still be congruent with the point of view of writers, such as Bandura and Douvan and Adelson, who deny the existence of any overt conflict, if the following are borne in mind.

First, there is the problem of method; one should not expect studies using different methods necessarily to produce the same results, and it is quite probable that an interview approach and the technique used here will elicit different types of material. Second, there are problems of design; comparisons should only be made between studies using similar samples, and this applies particularly to the age range of the subjects involved. In addition distinctions obviously cannot be drawn between the two sexes where dissimilar age groups have been included, and this is of especial importance in the consideration of Douvan and Adelson's work. Finally it is not necessarily inconsistent to find broad attitudinal similarities between generations, while at the same time discovering expressions of antipathy between individuals. The agreement between generations in their fundamental values does not rule out a very considerable degree of interpersonal conflict within families.

In looking at the present findings there is no doubt that the 'storm and stress' approach has provided an enormously helpful orientation in understanding the nature of adolescent relationships. However, two modifications may be mentioned which would bring this particular theory closer to the empirical evidence. First, it has been noted that conflict and tension are qualitatively different for boys and girls, and the nature of the issues expressed in the material indicates that such problems will not always be easy to articulate, especially for girls. In fact it is quite possible to envisage that in the case of many individuals such feelings will never reach the surface. Thus whatever notions of disruption or conflict there are need both to be elaborated and at all times carefully qualified. Second, the developmental sequence must be given further consideration. Although there are no explicit assumptions to be found within this approach, the implication is that disruption occurs contemporaneously in all areas. Such an implication gives rise to a visual image of the sort shown in figure 8.3.

While there are undoubted merits in this approach it can be seen that further differentiation is essential. The model which would be most consistent with the data presented here is that based on a stage theory approach. Such a theory revolves around

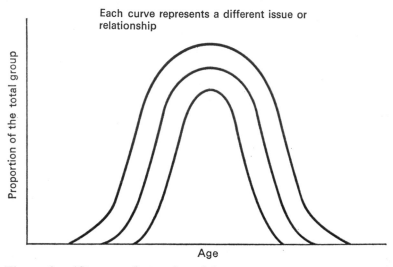

Figure 8.3 *'Storm and stress' model*

the notion of a sequence of distinctive and identifiable ages at which individuals undergo certain experiences and express specific types of behaviour. It has been noted that validation of a stage theory requires evidence relating both to the existence of limits or boundaries, as well as to factors common to a majority of the population within a particular stage. Initially writers taking this approach placed considerable emphasis upon distinctions between stages, and with regard to adolescence people such as Deutsch and Blos in his early writings perceived this period as a sequence of sub-stages, classified as early adolescence, adolescence proper, and late adolescence (Blos, 1962). However, it will be recalled that in his later writing Blos expressed some dissatisfaction with such a rigid categorization, and he is supported in this by Elkind's work on cognitive development. Both these writers seem happier to view adoles-

cence as a single stage within the whole sequence of development, with a series of different themes running through the
particular period.

With regard to the present study the findings reviewed in the
earlier part of the chapter indicate the existence of three
patterns, each of which appears to be specific to the various
stages of adolescent development. In early adolescence parents
and authority figures are valued, while solitude and heterosexual relationships appear as conflictful. In the middle stage
heterosexual relationships are idealized, while peer group situations and parental relationships for girls cause anxiety. Finally
solitude and the ability to be independent are perceived as positive, while future identity, authority in a group setting, and
parental relationships for boys are sources of conflict. Undeniably
these configurations illustrate three fairly discrete patterns which
would be congruent with a stage theory model of development.
However there are certain assumptions, explicit particularly in
the work of Freud and Piaget, which do not fit easily with the
present evidence. First, stage theory implies an invariant
sequence in which one stage follows another, the first being a
prerequisite for the next, and so on. Now in the present case the
results do not necessarily support this idea. There can be no
certainty that one stage always precedes another, and it is
possible to envisage for some adolescents the simultaneous
occurrence of two or even more of the patterns delineated here.
Such an issue could only be satisfactorily resolved by a longitudinal study. Of equal importance is the fact that stage theory
has a definite rigidity about it. The presence of boundaries is
assumed, as well as a relatively specific differentiation between
stages, yet the indications are that this is not the way things
happen. A model which takes account of the phenomena ob-
served in this study must be flexible, it must be able to contain
a certain degree of fluidity, and stage theory does not create an
impression of this sort. The image which comes to mind is of the
model illustrated in figure 8.4, which is in some ways very close
to the present approach, but is in some ways still very different.

The point of view taken in the present study is that adolescence is a single stage, as suggested by Blos and Elkind, but
that inherent within that stage are a number of separate
patterns. These patterns are distinctive in the descriptive sense,

but they are extremely flexible, they overlap and at times probably even co-exist in the developmental sense. In searching for an appropriate model of adolescent development it has been clear that the feature needing to take precedence over all others is the fact that at different ages particular sorts of relationship patterns come into focus, in the sense of being most prominent, but that no pattern appears to be specific to one age only. It is for this reason that the term focus has been employed, since it

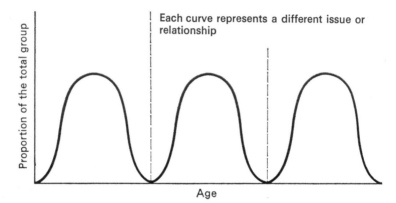

Figure 8.4 *Stage theory model*

reflects precisely this feature of the situation. Focus means firstly a centre, a pivot, a core, a point upon which attention converges. It also means, however, to make visible, to make clear, to bring into view something that has been present but outside the range of vision. It is in both these senses that a *focal* model of adolescent development is proposed. Graphically represented it would appear as shown in figure 8.5.

It will be apparent that, in symbolic form, the model illustrates simply the graphs already presented in this book superimposed upon each other. Thus the model faithfully represents the empirical evidence, giving the impression of developmental progression, of flexibility, and of overlap between patterns. Different issues come into focus at different times, but simply because an issue is not the most prominent feature of an age does not mean that it may not be critical for some individuals. The model is based upon and emerges out of evidence on a large group of adolescents. However there is no reason why it should

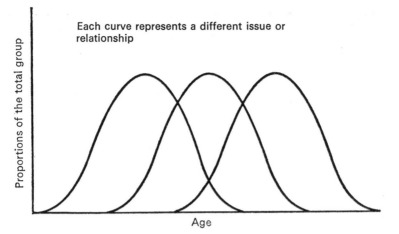

Figure 8.5 *Focal model*

not represent the progress of one individual through adolescence. Thus certain issues may be particularly pressing for a boy or girl at certain times, but other issues will not have disappeared; they will only have receded, remaining as residual sources of anxiety or conflict for quite long periods of time. Naturally the focal model illustrated above is a modal one, but any number of possible adolescent patterns may be envisaged. For example a group of delinquent or disturbed adolescents may look like this:

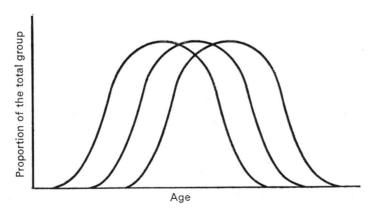

Figure 8.6 *Focal model of an atypical group*

Alternatively if the model was to represent one individual the progress of an adolescent who is a late developer might look like this:

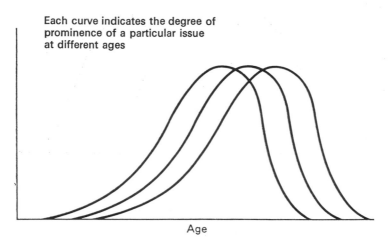

Figure 8.7 *Focal model of a late developer*

In an earlier chapter dissatisfaction was expressed with the state of adolescent psychology and some of the essentials for adequate research design, and therefore for models of adolescence, were spelled out. At that stage the most important features of a satisfactory approach were deemed to be a developmental and interactional dimension. However, in the course of this study the discovery of so much contiguity and overlap between relationship patterns has grown in consequence, and looking back it may now be argued that there is a further essential feature which must be incorporated into a concept of adolescence, namely a focal element. At the same time it is important to stress that the focal model has not been envisaged as an exclusive or all-embracing one, and there is no implication that, for example, the interactional point of view is henceforth redundant. The fact is that such a model is already well established, and is reflected to a degree in the role theory approach that has been considered here. The focal model, however, introduces a quite different dimension into the theory of adolescent development, and thus it has been proposed, not as an attempt to provide the final solution, but in the hope of contributing a new and more productive orientation to the developmental process.

Inevitably certain criteria must be applied to any psychological model; and in particular it is essential to consider whether it fits the data, and to what degree it is heuristic, in the sense of leading to further predictions. As far as the first is concerned, the focal model has been derived directly from the empirical evidence, so that it certainly fits the data presented here. Of course there may be other data with which the model is not consistent, but in this study a large proportion of the available evidence has been examined, and explanations have been suggested as to the resolution of some of the major controversies.

With regard to the second issue, while much further work needs to be done, a number of obvious predictions do follow from the model, all of which are amenable to testing. The most conspicuous example is that evidence from a longitudinal study should illustrate the same pattern of development. Next, different groups of adolescents will be expected to differ in the time course of their development, so that, as has been pictured above, graphs will vary depending on factors such as cultural background, early childhood experiences, and so on. Another important prediction is that pathology will be manifested in different ways, and will be easily identifiable within the model. Two possibilities, as we have seen, are that there might be too much overlap between stages, or alternatively that development will be excessively skewed to either end of the graph. Last, it is probable that the experience of specific situations will affect the temporal sequence. Interesting possibilities of investigation here are comparisons between adolescents in single sex and co-educational schools, or between those in boarding and day schools.

It will be recalled that one of the major aims of the study has been to show that empirical research can be relevant to everyday problems, and therefore one further criterion, possibly the most important of all, concerns the question of whether the model is helpful in promoting further understanding for those who are most directly involved with adolescents. With reference to these concerns the study has provided a number of significant pointers. In the first place, adolescent behaviour has been shown to be an on-going process rather than a series of isolated events caused by a bad mood, a row with the teacher, or whatever it is. In addition, behaviour is probably much more consistent than it appears to the individual observer, for the reason that one person, whoever that is, only sees a fragment of the total pattern. Furthermore, the research has indicated that large numbers of adolescents express similar types of behaviour at similar times during their development, so that one individual's difficulties need to be seen against the background of adolescence in general.

All these points are illustrated by the focal model. To begin with, the model underlines the continuity of adolescent relationships, showing that interaction at one moment in time is closely connected to both past and future. In particular it has been demonstrated that problem behaviour, as expressed in conflicts, disagreements or confrontations of one sort or another, is not just 'a stage', but the visible manifestation of a whole process of readjustment which began well before and will continue long after the specific happening which first drew the attention of the observer. Second, the model incorporates a notion of equivalence, in the sense that relationships in one area are balanced by relationships in another. Thus at different times separate issues come to the fore, although all are part of a total pattern. For example parents who experience a particularly difficult phase may find this much easier to cope with if they can envisage a process in which equivalent problems are expressed at different times in a wide range of relationships, rather than believing that the difficulties are their sole concern, and that the hostility, or whatever it is, is directed exclusively at them. Finally the model strongly suggests a common experience of the adolescent period. Clearly large numbers of young people from different backgrounds in different schools have, at various ages, much the same feelings and attitudes about relationships, and in fact the derivation of a focal model would not have been possible had this not been so. It seems essential to recognize therefore that in their contact with adolescents individual parents and teachers face problems which, while they are unique in some senses, have a general character which must make them easier to comprehend.

In conclusion, it is important to reiterate that adolescence is a complex period, and it has not been the intention in considering models of development to oversimplify the intricacy and irregularity of the process of maturation in young people. It is precisely for this reason that so much qualitative material has been included, in order that the idiosyncrasy of the individual personality should not be obscured. However, as developmental psychologists in the widest sense of that term, we must be involved in trying to clarify fundamental features of growth and change, and it has been to that end that a focal model of adolescent development has been proposed.

Appendix A

Table A *Total sample numbers, with mean ages for each group*

Age	Boys	(mean age in years and months)	Girls	(mean age in years and months)
11	102	(11.6)	114	(11.6)
13	95	(13.5)	110	(13.7)
15	79	(15.7)	96	(15.6)
17	71	(17.7)	72	(17.6)
Total	347		392	

Table B *Sample distribution in each school*

	Boys	Girls
School A (Public school)	75	—
School B (Public school)	—	94
School C (Grammar school-Inner London borough)	86	92
School D (Grammar school-Home Counties)	87	—
School E (Grammar school-Home Counties)	—	104
School F (Comprehensive school-Home Counties)	99	102
Total	347	392

Table C *Social class distribution amongst the total sample expressed in percentages*

Social class[1]	U.K. population 1966[2]	Present school sample
I	2.9	8·7
II	14·6	25·4
III	49·1	44·2
IV	22·3	13·1
V	8·0	3·9
Not classified	3·0	4·6

[1] Based on *Classification of Occupations*. Office of Population Censuses and Surveys, HMSO, 1970.
[2] Taken from *Social Trends*, HMSO, 1966.

Appendix B

Two tests have been used in the present study. In order of presentation the first consists of a series of pictures contained in a booklet handed to each subject. Opposite each picture is a blank page upon which the individual was asked to write his response. The actual instructions given are as follows:

In this booklet there are ten pictures. You will be asked to write a story about each of the pictures telling: (1) Who the people are; (2) What they're doing; and (3) How it's going to turn out. There is space to write on inside the booklet. You will have a definite time—about four minutes —for each picture, so do not turn over to the next one until you are told to do so.

For copyright reasons it has not been possible to print all the pictures used in the booklet. However, two which were drawn specially for this research are shown here to illustrate the type of material involved. These are picture 2 and picture 5. The rest are fully described below.

PICTURE I
Card A1 from *The Object Relations Technique* (Phillipson, 1955). This shows, in the middle foreground, an upright human figure in silhouette in slightly darker shading than the rest of the picture. In the left foreground is a darker patch of shading, often seen as a second figure. The shading is broken by patches of light around both figures and in the top of the picture.

PICTURE 2
As illustrated.

Picture 2

Picture 5

PICTURE 3
Card C3 from *The Object Relations Technique*. This shows an interior of a room in which are sketched three figures. One stands at the mantelpiece while the other two face each other across a table. The figures are ambiguous as to age and sex, but the two seated are often seen as being older than the one standing.

PICTURE 4
Card BG from *The Object Relations Technique*. This is an outdoor setting showing a structure in which there are two arches. The structure stretches away into the distance and a group of figures is to be seen in one arch, while in the other is standing one solitary individual. The impression of strong sunlight is given by shadows on the ground.

PICTURE 5
As illustrated.

PICTURE 6
Card A3 from *The Object Relations Technique*. Again an outdoor scene showing, on the right, the silhouettes of two figures almost touching, one being slightly taller than the other. On the left of the picture is a third figure standing out slightly from the light shading. Diagonally from left to right the shading gives an effect which is often interpreted as a road or stream separating the two figures from the third.

PICTURE 7
Drawn specially for the study. The picture shows a child just about to get into bed with an older person appearing at the doorway of the bedroom.

PICTURE 8
Card CG from *The Object Relations Technique*. This shows a long stairway covering almost the whole of the picture. On the top in the left corner is the shadow of a figure over the top three steps, and in the bottom right corner a group from which three or four figures are often distinguished, one of whom has an arm raised.

PICTURE 9
Card B2 from *The Object Relations Technique*. This shows an outdoor situation, with a house in the middle distance and two figures who are very close sheltering under a large tree in the foreground. The tree, the figures and the house are all in very dark shading, giving the impression of dusk or a storm.

PICTURE 10
Card 14 from the *Thematic Apperception Test* (Murray, 1943). This shows the silhouette of a figure against a bright window, with the rest of the picture entirely black. The figure could be entering or leaving the room, or could be just sitting on the windowsill.

The sentence-completion test was devised by the author specifically for the study. A considerable amount of pretesting was carried out, as well as a formal piece of research (Coleman, 1970). The instructions for the test are as follows:
Complete these unfinished sentences as quickly as you can. For example if the sentence was 'PEOPLE IN A GROUP . . . ' you might write 'are often good friends'. There are no right or wrong answers, just put down whatever seems to you to fit best.
The form for boys and girls differs slightly, as set out below.

Boy's form of sentence-completion test

1. USUALLY WHEN A BOY IS WITH HIS MOTHER . . .
2. IF SOMEONE IS NOT PART OF THE GROUP . . .
3. OFTEN WHEN THREE PEOPLE ARE TOGETHER . . .
4. FOR A BOY PARENTS . . .
5. WHEN THERE IS NO ONE ELSE AROUND I . . .
6. A BOY AND A GIRL TOGETHER . . .
7. WHEN SOMEONE GIVES ORDERS TO A GROUP . . .
8. IF I AM WITH TWO OTHER PEOPLE . . .
9. OFTEN A BOY AND HIS FATHER . . .
10. SOMETIMES WHEN I THINK ABOUT MYSELF . . .
11. FOR A BOY GIRLS . . .
12. IF A PERSON IS ALONE . . .
13. WHEN A BOY IS WITH HIS PARENTS . . .

14.   NOW AND AGAIN I REALIZE THAT I . . .

Girl's form of sentence-completion test

1.   USUALLY WHEN A GIRL IS WITH HER FATHER . . .
2.   IF SOMEONE IS NOT PART OF THE GROUP . . .
3.   OFTEN WHEN THREE PEOPLE ARE TOGETHER . . .
4.   FOR A GIRL PARENTS . . .
5.   WHEN THERE IS NO ONE ELSE AROUND I . . .
6.   A GIRL AND A BOY TOGETHER . . .
7.   WHEN SOMEONE GIVES ORDERS TO A GROUP . . .
8.   IF I AM WITH TWO OTHER PEOPLE . . .
9.   OFTEN A GIRL AND HER MOTHER . . .
10.   SOMETIMES WHEN I THINK ABOUT MYSELF . . .
11.   FOR A GIRL BOYS . . .
12.   IF A PERSON IS ALONE . . .
13.   WHEN A GIRL IS WITH HER PARENTS . . .
14.   NOW AND AGAIN I REALIZE THAT I . . .

Appendix C

As has been noted in the text, in all cases the initial analysis has been carried out with respect to Constructive, Negative, Neutral and Ambivalent themes. In addition there is in all groups a proportion of responses which have been classified as unscorable, either because of deliberate clowning, or because of the idiosyncratic nature of the material. For each test a scoring manual has been constructed. These have not been included, but are available from the author on request.

Where Constructive, Negative and Neutral themes are concerned *chi square* has been used to determine the levels of statistical significance in differences between age groups, and also where comparisons have been made between the two sexes. Both types of analysis are set out in the following tables. In view of the very large number of *chi square* tests which have been used, only those having a probability of less than 0·01 have been considered to be acceptable from the point of view of statistical significance.

Interjudge reliability is obviously of great importance in a situation such as the present one, where many untried scoring categories are being used. Two experienced clinical psychologists who had no connection with the administration of the tests were responsible for the scoring, all of which was done blind. In the case of all categories prior practice was given in scoring material, and categories were only used once an acceptable level of reliability had been reached. Once again further details may be obtained from the author if required.

It may be noted that in the following tables where the proportions of boys (B) and girls (G) in one age group have been

bracketed together a difference statistically significant beyond
the 0·01 level is indicated.

*Percentages of groups expressing
Constructive, Negative and Neutral themes*

Solitude

		11 yrs	*13 yrs*	*15 yrs*	*17 yrs*	*p*
Sentence 5						
Con.	B	3	6	18	25	<0·001
	G	12	12	27	36	<0·001
Neg.	B	25	13	11	12	N.S.
	G	24	15	15	13	N.S.
Neut.	B	70	78	61	55	N.S.
	G	56	69	55	44	<0·01
Sentence 12						
Con.	B	6	11	16	33	<0·001
	G	17	15	27	38	<0·01
Neg.	B	54	37	39	28	<0·01
	G	45	40	28	17	<0·001
Neut.	B	31	45	29	27	N.S.
	G	26	22	24	15	N.S.

Self-image

		11 yrs	*13 yrs*	*15 yrs*	*17 yrs*	*p*
Picture 10						
Con.	B	14	10	10	18	N.S.
	G	21	18	18	19	N.S.
Neg.	B	27	23	44	45	<0·01
	G	20	35	42	50	<0·001
Neut.	B	28	28	16	13	N.S.
	G	16	21	26	17	N.S.
Sentence 10						
Con.	B	24	23	23	13	N.S.
	G	16	15	13	15	N.S.
Neg.	B	29	44	35	25⎫	N.S.
	G	35	38	50	50⎭	N.S.
Neut.	B	27	20	33	28	N.S.
	G	31	25	25	22	N.S.
Sentence 14						
Con	B	31	24	25	22	N.S.
	G	28	25	23	28	N.S.
Neg.	B	30	35	35	36	N.S.
	G	30	31	43	32	N.S.
Neut.	B	17	11	21	10	N.S.
	G	17	12	9	7	N.S.

Heterosexual

		11 yrs	13 yrs	15 yrs	17 yrs	p
Picture 2						
Con.	B	39	59	71	61	<0·001
	G	45	60	64	60	N.S.
Neg.	B	7	15	12	12	N.S.
	G	9	11	13	11	N.S.
Neut.	B	48	22	10	16	<0·001
	G	39	29	21	28	N.S.
Picture 9						
Con.	B	24	28	39	22	N.S.
	G	26	23	42	40	<0·01
Neg.	B	3	10	13	12	N.S.
	G	77	13	14	8	N.S.
Neut.	B	44	38	29	31	N.S.
	G	44	45	32	35	N.S.
Sentence 6						
Con.	B	35	29	37	52	N.S.
	G	33	44	56	44	N.S.
Neg.	B	15	12	4	3	N.S.
	G	9	9	4	6	N.S.
Neut.	B	40	41	39	30	N.S.
	G	43	27	18	24	<0·001
Sentence 11						
Con.	B	27	42	52	52	<0·01
	G	19	41	53	43	<0·001
Neg.	B	37⎫	16	13⎫	6	<0·001
	G	23⎭	14	2⎭	14	<0·001
Neut.	B	10	16	19	15	N.S.
	G	16	9	8	10	N.S.

Two-person—parent

		11 yrs	*13 yrs*	*15 yrs*	*17 yrs*	*p*
Picture 5						
Con.	B	32	25	18	9	<0·01
	G	27	23	15	22	N.S.
Neg.	B	13	30	37	58	<0·001
	G	18	38	45	42	<0·001
Neut.	B	25	15	18	9	N.S.
	G	14	19	20	13	N.S.
Picture 7						
Con.	B	15	23	17	21	N.S.
	G	25	34	29	28	N.S.
Neg.	B	41	35	35	43	N.S.
	G	36	37	38	44	N.S.
Neut.	B	34	26	25	19	N.S.
	G	22	21	15	4	<0·01
Sentence 2 (Opposite sex)						
Con.	B	34	24	25	24⎫	N.S.
	G	19	27	40	44⎭	<0·001
Neg.	B	13	21	25	30	N.S.
	G	18	28	29	25	N.S.
Neut.	B	44	49	39	34	N.S.
	G	55	36	24	19	<0·001
Sentence 9 (Same sex)						
Con.	B	34	41	34	25⎫	N.S.
	G	33	51	53	50⎭	N.S.
Neg.	B	6	8	19	37	<0·001
	G	8	20	25	31	<0·001
Neut.	B	54	42	32	21	<0·001
	G	27	21	9	8	<0·001

Three-person—parent

		11 yrs	*13 yrs*	*15 yrs*	*17 yrs*	*p*
Picture 6						
Con.	B	18	24	6	18	N.S.
	G	25	16	8	14	N.S.
Neg.	B	36	45	56	48	N.S.
	G	46	55	56	56	N.S.
Neut.	B	29	15	20	10	<0·01
	G	16	22	25	18	N.S.
Sentence 4						
Con.	B	44	39	22⎤	28	<0·01
	G	47	39	42⎦	43	N.S.
Neg.	B	29	26	35	33	N.S.
	G	18	22	24	17	N.S.
Neut.	B	7	6	15	6	N.S.
	G	5	6	1	3	*
Sentence 13						
Con.	B	23	18	13	6⎤	N.S.
	G	23	19	18	28⎦	N.S.
Neg.	B	18	20⎤	39	58⎤	<0·001
	G	13	39⎦	45	35⎦	<0·001
Neut.	B	51	42	23	18	<0·001
	G	46	24	16	7	<0·001

* Not calculated

Three-person—friendship

		11 yrs	*13 yrs*	*15 yrs*	*17 yrs*	*p*
Picture 3						
Con.	B	21	21	20	22	N.S.
	G	19	16	19	31	N.S.
Neg.	B	7	24	39	24	<0·001
	G	7	31	52	28	<0·001
Neut.	B	60	51	30	33	<0·001
	G	44	42	22	35	<0·01
Sentence 3						
Con.	B	23	16	11	15	N.S.
	G	19	14	7	17	N.S.
Neg.	B	29⎞	56	62⎞	57	<0·001
	G	50⎠	71	80⎠	68	<0·001
Neut.	B	46	27	23	21	<0·001
	G	28	14	7	15	<0·001
Sentence 8						
Con.	B	18	16	15	15	N.S.
	G	20	13	19	21	N.S.
Neg.	B	14	16⎞	15⎞	15	N.S.
	G	20	32⎠	35⎠	25	N.S.
Neut.	B	56	52	47	39	N.S.
	G	42	34	22	40	N.S.

Large group—rejection

		11 yrs	13 yrs	15 yrs	17 yrs	p
Picture 4						
Con.	B	2	5	11	24	<0·001
	G	3	10	18	26	<0·001
Neg.	B	17	40	51	34	<0·001
	G	25	39	47	36	N.S.
Neut.	B	70	46	29	33	<0·001
	G	63	45	31	32	<0·001
Sentence 2						
Con.	B	5	2	1	15	*
	G	4	3	9	15	<0·01
Neg.	B	70	79	71	42	<0·001
	G	75	76	68	58	N.S.
Neut.	B	22	14	22	25	N.S.
	G	13	11	11	10	N.S.

* Not calculated

Large group—authority

		11 yrs	13 yrs	15 yrs	17 yrs	p
Picture 8						
Con.	B	5	10	6	13	N.S.
	G	9	10	6	6	N.S.
Neg.	B	31	45	41	55	N.S.
	G	35	44	50	61	<0·01
Neut.	B	35	23	22	7	<0·001
	G	32	25	20	14	N.S.
Sentence 7						
Con.	B	46	17	18	9	<0·001
	G	33	12	17	7	<0·001
Neg.	B	32	59	52	60	<0·001
	G	20	46	58	61	<0·001
Neut.	B	16	7	9	12	N.S.
	G	30	16	9	10	<0·001

Appendix D

While many individual stories and sentences have been quoted in the course of this book, there has been no opportunity to present full protocols of individual adolescents. Since many of these are of such interest it seemed a great pity not to include at some stage a small selection of records. These have been chosen as representative of an age group, rather than because they are particularly amusing, peculiar or idiosyncratic, and one boy and one girl have been used to illustrate the eleven-, thirteen-, fifteen- and seventeen-year age groups. In fact the selection process amongst the seventeen-year-olds proved so difficult that in the end two boys and girls from this age group have been included—one seventeen- and one eighteen-year-old. No further comment is necessary—the records speak for themselves.

Boys

Eleven-year-old boy, who has one younger brother, and whose father is a building contractor.

Picture-story test

PICTURE I
This could be someone standing on a soap box or something and talking or lecturing to a crowd of people. It could turn out by him getting off his stand and being patted on his back by the crowd as he walks to his car.

PICTURE 2
This could be a boy who has returned late from hunting in the mountains and his mother was worried. How she is glad to see him back again. Or two people who want to get married but their parents won't allow it so they have to meet each other at night. In the end the parents consent to the marriage.

PICTURE 3
Two people are having a meal and they have an argument about their son and then their son comes in the room and finds that they have been arguing and he wonders what he has done wrong. In the end his parents tell him and he apologises.

PICTURE 4
This is an abstract painting telling us what happened after a town had been struck by an earthquake. This shows some of the survivors who have gathered together to discuss how they are going to rebuild the town. Soon they get help and they build the new town.

PICTURE 5
Mothers day. Son and father wait for Mother to come out of her bedroom and then they give her their presents. Or it could be two burglars waiting outside a rich womans hotel room waiting for her to come out so that they could rob her.

PICTURE 6
A small boy has just become king of a country and the other two men are members of parliament presenting themselves to the king. They are very nice to him so as they can get a rise of pay. Any other king would know that they were sucking up to him but as he is so young he does not understand.

PICTURE 7
The father sends his child to bed early and when he comes upstairs to see if the child had gone to bed and when he gets upstairs he finds that the child has put his clothes on and is just about to climb out of the window. He hits the child and sends him back to bed and tells him that he will have to go to bed early for the rest of the year.

PICTURE 8
Some people standing at the bottom of a flight of stairs waiting for someone famous to come out of a building at the top. Soon he comes out and the man in the top left hand corner is his shadow.

PICTURE 9
Some people playing cricket against a tree, using it as a wicket. One of the people is the batsman, the other the wicket keeper. Soon they have to pack up and they go home to the flats where they live (in the background).

PICTURE 10
A man climbed up the drainpipe. He opened the window and climbed in. He put all his things he had stolen in a bag and threw the bag to a man waiting down below. Then he climbed out of the window, scrambled down the drainpipe and was off in a car in hardly any time at all.

Sentence-completion test
 1.   USUALLY WHEN A BOY IS WITH HIS MOTHER he is well behaved.
 2.   IF SOMEONE IS NOT PART OF THE GROUP he will do anything to try and join it.
 3.   OFTEN WHEN THREE PEOPLE ARE TOGETHER they have better fun than if they were alone.
 4.   FOR A BOY PARENTS look after him.
 5.   WHEN THERE IS NO ONE ELSE AROUND I like to do things out of the ordinary.
 6.   A BOY AND A GIRL TOGETHER usually have *lots* of fun.
 7.   WHEN SOMEONE GIVES ORDERS TO A GROUP the group accept them.
 8.   IF I AM WITH TWO OTHER PEOPLE I like to be the boss.
 9.   OFTEN A BOY AND HIS FATHER does jobs such as mending a plug or something masculine.
 10.   SOMETIMES WHEN I THINK ABOUT MYSELF I think I am not as good as I think I am.
 11.   FOR A BOY GIRLS will do anything.
 12.   IF A PERSON IS ALONE he is usually melancholy.

13.   WHEN A BOY IS WITH HIS PARENTS he is also well behaved.
14.   NOW AND AGAIN I REALIZE THAT I am rather disobedient.

Thirteen-year-old boy, who has one younger brother, and whose father is a shop steward in a timber factory.

Picture-story test

PICTURE 1
There is a man in the picture about middle-aged, tall, and very strong looking. He seems to be standing in between a crowd of pupils or people talking to them. It seems as if it is going to turn out that the discussion which they are having is an interesting one, and that the pupils or people are asking many questions. (In the picture, by the way he is standing) it seems to me that he is just getting down deep into a question and trying to answer it.

PICTURE 2
There are two people in the picture, a man, and a woman. It seems to me that the woman has just come out of the house and is greeting the man in front of the door. It seems as if she is upset and has come to him for help. She might be asking him to take her far away from this horrid house where she is having many rows with her parents. The man don't seem to be agreeing with all this and says he can't do it because it would be wrong. He then goes home.

PICTURE 3
Here in this picture are two old lady's sitting down around a fire drinking cups of tea and swapping conversation for one to the other. It seems as if the one nearest the front is trieing to explain something to the one further back (who has her hand up to her face) but she don't really want to know so she takes no notise. Then finely the talkative lady leaves and the quite lady says to herself 'thank goodness' for that.

PICTURE 4
Here are a group of boys in the street a gang if you like. Now there is a crowd of boys talking on the left hand side are saying

nasty things about the solitary boy on the right. It seems to me that the gang of boys are ignoring the other boy and not talking to him. Now the boy by himself has been left out through his own fault because he told on the boys when they broke a car window. Then the crowd of boys are going to jump him and beat him up for doing it.

PICTURE 5
In this picture there a father and his son talking seriously. Now the father has been informed that his son has been rather bad at school, and is giving him a telling off. The boy knowing he has done wrong admits everything. So the father sends the son into his room without any supper (instead of beating him) and locks the door. In the picture the door is half open. At this point the boy has just been told his punishment.

PICTURE 6
In this picture I can see a man, and a woman about to be married by the vicor standing on the left. They are now repeating their vows and are almost through now. After the wedding their is to be a big reception in the church hall, where the bride and groom cut the big 3 storey cake.

PICTURE 7
Here is a relapse of a storee before where the father and son had a talk about the boys behavior. Now the father has thought to himself that prehaps the boy cound't help it has come up to his room where he is just getting into bed to give him something to eat. But the boy doesn't want it and jumps into bed with his hanki in his hand (for he has a bad cold) and just tells his father to go away. So he does.

PICTURE 8
In this picture it looks like a tale from Greek Mithology, where there are four bad men who have gone against the word of one of the god's. And from the blacked angry sky comes one of the god's. The four men are terrified and trie to get away, but it is to late the god just sent lightning after them to banish them to another universe for ever.

PICTURE 9

In this picture there is a man and a woman. They are standing under a large tree and talking. They plan to run away together because they are in love. Then the man and the woman kiss and they part to go and get ready for the journey. But their plans were soon going to be stopped by the womans husband who shoots the womans lover. Now the woman kills herself and the husband is left all alone.

PICTURE 10

There is a boy standing at a window just waiting to get out. He is in a boarding school and wants to run away home to his mother (who didn't want him to go there in the first place). So he climbs out the window, down the drainpipe and hitchhikes home. But his father finds out and sends him back. And now back at the boarding school he looks up at the sky and stars and thinks of his mother.

Sentence-completion test

1. USUALLY WHEN A BOY IS WITH HIS MOTHER he has no friends to play with.
2. IF SOMEONE IS NOT PART OF THE GROUP he usually tries to spoil it for the others.
3. OFTEN WHEN THREE PEOPLE ARE TOGETHER they tend to do things they would not do by themselves.
4. FOR A BOY PARENTS to be so hard on him, it is very wrong.
5. WHEN THERE IS NO ONE ELSE AROUND I have to go along otherwise I would be left out of everything.
6. A BOY AND A GIRL TOGETHER usually talk on only one thing.
7. WHEN SOMEONE GIVES ORDERS TO A GROUP they do it for the groups own benefit.
8. IF I AM WITH TWO OTHER PEOPLE I always do things I would never do by myself.
9. OFTEN A BOY AND HIS FATHER have good times for they both understand what things each other likes.
10. SOMETIMES WHEN I THINK ABOUT MYSELF I think that sometime I am very foolish.
11. FOR A BOY GIRLS crowd round him an awful lot.
12. IF A PERSON IS ALONE they are very unhappy.

13.   WHEN A BOY IS WITH HIS PARENTS he is very good and hardly steps out of line.

14.   NOW AND AGAIN I REALIZE THAT I should do things for people more often.

Fifteen-year-old boy who has two older brothers, and whose father is an actuary.

Picture-story test

PICTURE 1
There is a man of about thirty who has gone for a walk over a dull and misty common. On the way he begins to think about his life and about his family. He soon becomes lost in thought and quite unaware of the cold bleak common surrounding him. He eventually reaches home tired and worried.

PICTURE 2
A newly-married couple are going for a walk in the surrounding countryside where they hope to find peace and tranquility. They talk about the future they hope to have and how they are going to arrange their lives. They return to the house with new ideas and aspirations.

PICTURE 3
An old couple living alone far from the crowds and bustle of the city. They have just had dinner and the husband has got up for his tobacco and pipe in order to relax in his armchair and contemplate his life and appreciate the love of his wife. The couple talk for many hours.

PICTURE 4
A school-outing to an old ruined monastry. The boys are talking amongst themselves about the scenery. One boy is unpopular, either because he is coloured or uninteresting and is excluded from the rest of the boys. Even the master in the middle lacks interest in the boy. They will continue to do so.

PICTURE 5
A father wanting his son to mix more with people is taking him

to a party but wishes to show that boy is not forced to go but wishes to go himself so he stands to one side of the door. The boy has always been shy and is dreading the next few hours until his father picks him up. It will turn out better than the boy expected having realized people are not so bad.

PICTURE 6
The people are two parents and their son going out for a sunday-afternoon walk. The boy is used not to walking with his parents and is worried in case his friends see him and so stands a little way away pretending not to know them. His parents are a definite embarrassment to him—he prefers people of his own generation. As he grows up the generation gap widens further.

PICTURE 7
A young daughter is just getting into bed tired after her active day when her father comes in to have a talk with her. She is annoyed but is ashamed to tell her father she is tired. He talks to her about her school-life which is unusual as he rarely takes an interest in her and she wonders if he is leading up to the facts of life which she knew 3 years ago.

PICTURE 8
An old church visited in the summer is open. It is a hot sunny day and the people are having a picnic at the bottom of the steps. The leave litter and are messing the place. An angry official is coming towards them down the steps preparing what his angry words will be. He knows they will not have much effect.

PICTURE 9
A middle-aged married couple have gone to Italy for their second honeymoon. They are trying desparately to recapture the atmosphere that they have lost from their first honeymoon but cannot make a success of it. They are going to get farther apart as they cannot find anything nice to say to each other. Only sarcastic remarks.

PICTURE 10
A man living alone is fed up with the life he leads and has decided

that there is no escape from it. Every day is the same mono-
tonous one as before. He is sitting on the window-sill contemplating suicide. He eventually decides that that is the only
answer although he tries desparately to find another way. He
throws himself off into another world.

Sentence-completion test

1.   USUALLY WHEN A BOY IS WITH HIS MOTHER he can find
some sort of comfort in her.

2.   IF SOMEONE IS NOT PART OF THE GROUP he feels totally
uncared for and unwanted.

3.   OFTEN WHEN THREE PEOPLE ARE TOGETHER they quarrel
about what is the best thing to do.

4.   FOR A BOY PARENTS often become an unwanted but necessary embarrassment.

5.   WHEN THERE IS NO ONE ELSE AROUND I think to myself
about my relationships with other people.

6.   A BOY AND A GIRL TOGETHER often find a mutual understanding between each other taking the place of their parents.

7.   WHEN SOMEONE GIVES ORDERS TO A GROUP many feel it
is not fair or he is going the wrong way about it.

8.   IF I AM WITH TWO OTHER PEOPLE I find I can talk to one
and the other gets left out.

9.   OFTEN A BOY AND HIS FATHER find an understanding but
sometimes an anoyance with the other one.

10.   SOMETIMES WHEN I THINK ABOUT MYSELF I wonder if this
is really the life I want to lead.

11.   FOR A BOY GIRLS are a dreaded fear, or an aggravation or
someone they can get on with.

12.   IF A PERSON IS ALONE he despairs.

13.   WHEN A BOY IS WITH HIS PARENTS he quarells with them.

14.   NOW AND AGAIN I REALIZE THAT I have said the wrong
thing at the wrong time and am sorry for it.

Seventeen-year-old boy, the oldest of a family of four, whose
father is a consulting engineer.

Picture-story test

PICTURE I
There is a man standing and with him there appear to be several

characters lying down on the ground. There looks to be one person kneeling over another one in one corner.

They appear to be in some sort of stupour or physically wounded state with one man or figure completely unharmed.

I think that the people lying about are wounded fighters of a cause and the figure standing up is their ideal—a form of social realism.

Perhaps they are communists wounded fighting fascism with the upright figure probably dressed in national costume. In fact there is no story as such to this picture.

PICTURE 2

There are two characters, probably one male and one female judging by physical appearance. They are standing by a path of a house looking out through the gate and at the big wide and wonderful world outside the gate.

The story will end with them making up their minds and stepping quickly along the path, out of the gate and forward to meet the world.

This has broader meanings; it could mean someone from the middle-class breaking out of the bourgeousie surroundings and searching for a different truth to the one he was brought up on.

PICTURE 3

There are three people in the room, all men.

One is standing facing a mirror while the other two are sitting down facing each other.

I think they have all been discussing a tricky problem, perhaps they are trying to decide whether to commit a robbery, or perhaps simply where to go on holiday, but they have definitely come to some point at which decision must be reached but has not been so far.

Presumably I am meant to note and develop, in conjunction with the story, the dark black object specially emphasised for the purpose. Perhaps I am simply meant to write a sentence like my last—Well, on both accounts you were lucky, at least partially.

PICTURE 4

There are a group of figures and then, further along, there is a solitary figure. The group appear to be talking together about something while the solitary figure is standing upright and alone.

The end of the story will be tragic, the group cannot long tolerate an individualist in their vicinity. His ideas might counter, or even shatter their own. Therefore he must go. This does not mean necessarily death but in whatever form it is tragic because of the lack of individualism present in our 'group 'world. Also it could be noted that there is much more light coming through the gap the solitary figure is silhouetted against.

PICTURE 5

There are two figures—a man and a boy, or possibly a woman & a girl but essentially two characters, one big, one small.

The big one is some way from an open door directly outside which is the small figure.

They seem to be contemplating the question of whether to go in but I don't believe this—'seems, I know not seems'. I believe they have left the room—perhaps they have moved away from a mother figure within. The small one regrets this most and hence is nearest the door, while the big one, although not equally regretful, does stop. It will end with them returning through the door, the way they came.

PICTURE 6

There are basically three characters here though there is a possibility of more. Two are facing a wall of some sort while the other is facing them. The two were the one's friends but he is of some opposite belief and he is going to shoot them. He is talking to them trying to put over his point of view and fortunately for him his friends are making it easier by standing up and taking it. He is in complete control and they don't say a word.

Eventually, when the one has sufficiently salved his conscience, he shoots the other two. He does the job well and does not create pain. He would probably advance to within two yards, shoot them both through the back of the head and depart.

PICTURE 7

There are two figures.

One is about to get into bed while the other is standing in the

door. She, on the bed, was waiting for him to come but he is slightly scared. The Graduate—he will come in to the room, overcome his fears, and make love to her, or rather let her make love to him.

I can imagine the bastard who thought this one up wanted everyone to make up tales of Jack & Jill going up the hill—well my friend you're wrong and if I had more time I could make this story make Frank Harris look like Noddy went to Toytown.

PICTURE 8

There are a group of people and one advancing from above. The group are sitting at the bottom of the steps—the steps of life— and the shadow is of one who will help these people to throw off their oppressors and rise for his own benefit.

This picture is one of Fascism—at the bottom are the German People—discontented revengeful, young—coming from above is Hitler with all his masterful eloquence and propaganda. He is coming to make these people fight—and die for HIM, not for themselves. He fills them with dreams and hopes, so easy to grab hold off if you are discontented, and then he pushes them gently over the edge of the abyss into war.

PICTURE 9

There are two figures shown. Again one large, one medium person. Possibly it is raining and they are standing under a tree and talking, probably of love. Maybe they're homosexuals, maybe lesbian, maybe heterosexuals.

Being an old romantic I think their affair is just about to crack up and despite the pleading of one the other is adamant. Knife flash, love triumphant, disgust and pity—perhaps.

They split and do their own thing—One passionate
One despairing
One crying
One dying.

PICTURE 10

One person silhoueted
The person is looking out of, climbing out of, climbing in

through a window. She came in through the bathroom window—
maybe.
The person can see light outside and only darkness inside but
this is not life
Life is the room, dark and repellent
Light is outside for him to grasp
Method for grasping is only too simple
A window opens—the way out appears
Death beyond the window
Sought for, looked for, pushed for, obtained
For him, the light, for so many the darkness

Sentence-completion test

1.   USUALLY WHEN A BOY IS WITH HIS MOTHER he is quite content until he gets older.

2.   IF SOMEONE IS NOT PART OF THE GROUP he should be proud of it if he can think, if not he smells.

3.   OFTEN WHEN THREE PEOPLE ARE TOGETHER one is going to get left out and the other two sods will be alright.

4.   FOR A BOY PARENTS are people who he should be able to turn to—I can't, bit of money maybe, bike looked after.

5.   WHEN THERE IS NO ONE ELSE AROUND I piss all over any wall I can find.

6.   A BOY AND A GIRL TOGETHER are very likely to have a bit of the other unless she's as tight as a clam—maybe rape.

7.   WHEN SOMEONE GIVES ORDERS TO A GROUP I resent it, get knackered for resenting it and resent it even more.

8.   IF I AM WITH TWO OTHER PEOPLE I never am friend.

9.   OFTEN A BOY AND HIS FATHER have fun.

10.   SOMETIMES WHEN I THINK ABOUT MYSELF I reckon either I'm a genius slow developing or I should commit suicide.

11.   FOR A BOY GIRLS are things for getting your kicks until you meet one, there's probably only one special, I haven't met her yet.

12.   IF A PERSON IS ALONE he should be happy—think about yourself, your problems and tell the world to piss off.

13.   WHEN A BOY IS WITH HIS PARENTS I never am, except for meals.

14.   NOW AND AGAIN I REALIZE THAT I am *really weird*.

Eighteen-year-old boy, the middle one in a family of three, whose father deals in reproduction antique furniture.

Picture-story test

PICTURE I
Shadowy—nonhuman being from depths of space. A visitor to earth, with ability to materialise & dematerialise at will. Conducting a survey into the habits of Earth creatures & coming to the conclusion that, in a few million years time man may be civilised, unless he has wiped himself out. Has vaguely human form. Can mingle in crowds etc without being noticed, but as an individual is easily recogniseable as non-human. When his survey is over he will quietly transport himself back home & noone will be the wiser on earth.

PICTURE 2
Two lovers—free & able to do as they please. Living in open country, but fenced in. The gate allows them to leave their own little world & reenter 'a civilised' community, but they are loathe to leave. The house is not their idea of an ideal house— detached houses & semidets. are found in any town, but is good enough—who wants to live in a cave anyway? They often stand together in silence gazing at the rising sun appearing from behind the mountains—another new day together.

PICTURE 3
Family life. The warmth of an open fire & a seemingly happy family gathered together after tea—but the son, standing by the fireplace is not too happy. His parents, sitting, looking at him are not aware he is now grown up. He wants to be independent, get away from parental grip—but the love of the family holds him back—the warmth of the fire is preferable, perhaps, to cold uncertainty outside. But one day he will break away & leave—although his parents will not be able to accept this at first.

PICTURE 4
One solitary figure, apart from the group of people standing in the other archway. He is exiled, banished from the tall walls

of the castle. Soon he will set off along the straight road into the sunset. And noone will see or hear from him again, though noone cares. Once he is removed from the group, they continue to exist as before—contented yet always in the shadow of the high battlements. Alone he can get away from the pillars of war & lose himself in the brilliant light of freedom & happiness— but first he must leave the walls behind him.

PICTURE 5
Unwilling to go through the door, to face whatever lies behind it. Punishment—the headmaster's cane. The pupil stands, afraid as the door opens & the prefect prepares to usher him in to meet his doom. The plants are still alive, but the arsenic & weed killer will soon take effect & they will die. Perhaps he deserves his punishment for killing the plants—though punishment will be dealt out before the full effect of his actions are felt by the plants. Meanwhile he must wait—& pray for forgiveness—but too late the door is opening.

PICTURE 6
Once again a solitary figure, but confronted by two nameless beings. He is asked to choose between the two, which one is his friend, which his enemy. Both face him with equal vagueness, smiling, hypocritical faces, beckoning him on to sorrow or joy. He seems to go for the one on the left & together they will go off into the middle distance where the darkness ends & joy begins. Obviously he has chosen right. The other being, foiled again, stands waiting for the next traveller—who will not be quite so lucky perhaps.

PICTURE 7
Father comes to put his daughter to bed. It is late, she has been allowed to stay up because it's her birthday but now it's bedtime. Silhouetted in the doorway daddy smiles at his daughter who happily clambers into bed. She has got a new dress, which she has just put away in the wardrobe, after having admired herself in the mirror. One day she will be grown up like mummy & have makeup she can wear & look in the mirror to see if its on right, but now she's just a tiny girl, and happy.

PICTURE 8
The shadow of an unknown man advancing on a frightened group of spectators brought suddenly out of the calm peace of everyday life, confronted with fear. Sitting in an amphitheatre, probably tourists. Suddenly the ghost of past civilisation appears from nowhere & they are unable to move, to act, to save themselves as the past approaches down the steps, slowly methodically until it reaches them, engulfs them & continues into the future. Retribution.

PICTURE 9
Loneliness in the centre of a city. An old couple, their lifes almost at an end stand in a city park—as far from the dull grimy buildings as they can get—seeking peace or rest. They are unable to leave the town, yet the park offers them some happiness. Every day they stand together beneath the tree, reminiscing. To-morrow they will do exactly the same thing, and the next day, until one day their bodies are found in their bed-sitting room on the top floor of the grey building—and the park will be empty that day—untill another old couple find rest beneath that tree.

PICTURE 10
'He believed he could fly', the newspapers said. He had fallen from an upper floor of a high building. He had sought the light, and found it, but failed to achieve much except a mess on the pavement below. His sleeve is rolled up, the syringe lies somewhere in the darkness, used, forgotten. Outside the prison of his room, the prison of his mind, lay the everlasting; the open window led to the night, so he found eternal rest, God help him.

Sentence-completion test
1. USUALLY WHEN A BOY IS WITH HIS MOTHER he is able to joke, be happy, but unable to communicate this mentally.
2. IF SOMEONE IS NOT PART OF THE GROUP he is possibly happier, finds it easier to think, but misses friendship.
3. OFTEN WHEN THREE PEOPLE ARE TOGETHER one is the odd one out.
4. FOR A BOY PARENTS are symbols of authority & sometimes unhappiness, but necessary links with 'society'.

5.   WHEN THERE IS NO ONE ELSE AROUND I feel free and able to think, rarely need others' company.

6.   A BOY AND A GIRL TOGETHER, provided they are attracted to each other, is an ideal state.

7.   WHEN SOMEONE GIVES ORDERS TO A GROUP, there is always one who refuses to obey.

8.   IF I AM WITH TWO OTHER PEOPLE, depending on their sex, etc. I sometimes feel not needed, sometimes a vital 3rd party.

9.   OFTEN A BOY AND HIS FATHER manage to get on together but sometimes quarrel.

10.   SOMETIMES WHEN I THINK ABOUT MYSELF I wonder why.

11.   FOR A BOY GIRLS in the plural are the opposite sex, but *a* girl is happiness.

12.   IF A PERSON IS ALONE he probably wishes to be so, but if not, he needs a friend.

13.   WHEN A BOY IS WITH HIS PARENTS there is often a lack of communication.

14.   NOW AND AGAIN I REALIZE THAT I have acted foolishly, but never regret my life so far.

Girls

Eleven-year-old girl who has two younger sisters, and whose father is a sales manager.

Picture-story test

PICTURE I
I see the shape of a man in the picture. It is a foggy day and he is walking through a park. He is very tall and is in fact a robber, he has been followed by the police who now unfortunately have been given the slip. The man thinks he is safe and proceeds to walk back on to . . .

PICTURE 2
A boy and girl are in this picture and they are going to say goodbye to each other outside the girl's house, for her parents will not let her boyfriend into the house, so they meet each other in secrecy. They had hoped to get married but their hopes had been dashed by the refusal of permission from the girls parents.

However they are planning to run away and get married secretly in Australia, which they did.

PICTURE 3
Bill was staying with his father and mother in a cottage in a village. Bill was staying because his wife had been killed in a car crash a few weeks ago and Bill had been so very upset that he had been ill and had been advised by his doctor to go and spend a few months by the sea. So he had naturally gone to his parents. Bill after a while went away to America where he lived quite contentedly.

PICTURE 4
This is an old temple somewhere in Greece. It has just been the scene of a murder in which a girl had been pushed done from an arch right at the top. The police knew she had been pushed because on her body there was also signs of a stabbing in her chest. The police have got some clues because of a scented handkerchief which had been left lying on the flat top. The police dogs, went after the scent and came back with the prisoner.

PICTURE 5
Paul Shimmer, was busy doing the paper round when he saw a man across the road, the man was fiddling with the door. Paul knew that Mrs. Porter who lived there was on holiday so he went over to ask the man what he was doing. The man said that he was from the gas company and was trying to see where Mrs. Sillen lived, Paul thought it peculiar, for the man not to know his name so he went home and phoned the police and the man was found out to be a burglar of high reputation.

PICTURE 6
It was a cold wet day and Tom Brown was going to play with his friends, Jim and Andy. The boys had their own camp, compiled of twigs and mainly was a hollow. The boys loved it and enjoyed playing there. When they reached it, Andy began to scrabble in the earth and his fingers touched a box but which contained something hard. Excited he digged away and at last pulled out a small sized sack. He opened it out and found jewels, which he took to the police and got a reward for his honesty.

PICTURE 7

Jack had been naughty and had been sent up to bed by his mother who had been annoyed with him. Jack hated this punishment and sulked until his father came in. Father went up to his room and gave Jack a lecture, but after that Jack was allowed downstairs to apologise to his mother and to his relieve enjoy an evening of television.

PICTURE 8

This picture reminds me of a play in which the cast at the bottom of the steps are villians and the shadow on the steps is their leader. They are planning a big jewellry robbery but the villans are planning to kill their leader and so have one less person to share the treasure with. But somehow or other the leader seemed to know and quietly slipped away never to return, the villans carried out the robbery, and luckily, were caught, but the leader was not found and no-one knows where he's hid.

PICTURE 9

In the grounds of the country mansion in the picture there is a huge tree which has been there ever since the foundation stone had been laid in the 19th century. It was a tall tree, and had stood through rain, snow, sun and wind. Now though it seemed as though it was to end its life for people wanted to cut it down. Two people oppossed them and they were the owners of the mansion. An elderly couple who had seen the tree stand there all their lifes. There was going to be a vote in the town hall.

PICTURE 10

I see a open window in the picture John had been late for boarding school and so in the course had been locked out. John saw an open window right at the top of the school and so he proceeds to climb up the wall aided by the Ivy and drainpipe which were there. Luckily John was able to get in without much trouble and so got back into his own dormitory without being seen but if he had been seen he would have suffered the consequences.

Sentence-completion test

✓1.   USUALLY WHEN A GIRL IS WITH HER FATHER she *ought* to behave.

2. IF SOMEONE IS NOT PART OF THE GROUP they are usually shy.

3. OFTEN WHEN THREE PEOPLE ARE TOGETHER they might make mischief.

4. FOR A GIRL PARENTS are there to be asked things.

5. WHEN THERE IS NO ONE ELSE AROUND I often talk to myself.

6. A GIRL AND A BOY TOGETHER usually like one another.

7. WHEN SOMEONE GIVES ORDERS TO A GROUP they should obey.

8. IF I AM WITH TWO OTHER PEOPLE I am usually shy.

9. OFTEN A GIRL AND HER MOTHER do a lot of things together.

10. SOMETIMES WHEN I THINK ABOUT MYSELF I sigh in disapproval.

11. FOR A GIRL BOYS are sometimes a nuisance.

12. IF A PERSON IS ALONE he might talk to himself.

13. WHEN A GIRL IS WITH HER PARENTS she should follow their *example* and remember things she will need to know.

14. NOW AND AGAIN I REALIZE THAT I am *sometimes* horrid to my sisters.

Thirteen-year-old girl with two younger brothers, whose father is a top-level civil servant.

Picture-story test

PICTURE I

These people are social outcasts. They may be squatters. The woman has a young baby. The man does all he can to maintain their rights and standard of living. I don't think they will find a home by themselves for quite a while, but somebody will come and help them.

I don't think it is their fault that they have ended up like this, they obviously don't know how it began or how it will end. The mother is sorry for her child and the father is sorry for the mother but neither can give either any help.

PICTURE 2

These people have just sold their house. They are standing in the garden looking at it and trying to recapture all the good and bad times they have had while they lived there. They want to take one lingering glance so that the memory of that house will stay with them forever. They are thinking they will never find another house they will love so well as they love this house. I think that perhaps when they are older they may come back and try to recapture the pleasant moments they had in the garden.

PICTURE 3
These people are discussing what they will do tomorrow. The one standing up and the one on the left are quite young and want to do different things. The Wise Uncle in the chair has decided that neither of them shall do what they wanted, and he will take them out. The one standing is looking scornfully at the other and is very pleased that he cannot do what he wanted to.

PICTURE 4
This is a group of school boys. One is very unhappy at school because he has no friends. It is in the playground and the boys are discussing wether to let him in and play their games. Most of the boys want to be friends with him but because their 'leader' has a grudge against him they do not want to speak to him and fall out with their leader. I think the boys will break away from the leader and eventually make friends.

PICTURE 5
The door has opened and the rubber plant is to be thrown out. The dominant father is fed up with having to move it from place to place when it gets in the way. The boy found this plant in a smashed pot somewhere and brought it home for fun. The plant will probably end up smashed again and practically die—it may be saved again though.

PICTURE 6
This is a game the boy on the left has got to choose who's fault it was, or who has got 'it'. He doesn't want to be too hasty because if he is wrong he is afraid his friends, behind him, will say he was stupid and it was quite obvious who had it. He has

to hurry to make his decision because the other boys want a go. The other boys are older & he thinks they will sneer at him if he gets it wrong. He guesses and just by chance he gets it right.

PICTURE 7
This young girl has just got out of bed to play with a toy. She did not notice her father at the doorway until he moved and she saw his shadow. She knows she has been naughty so now, as she scrambles back to bed, she is trying to think of an effective excuse. She will say her hot-water bottle fell out of bed or she spilt her water or something.

PICTURE 8
These people have not done anything wrong that they know of but they have said something they shouldn't have. They are being chased down the steps and are running for all they are worth, they don't know why but everyone else is running so they run too. They are frightened because when they look back with a glance they can only see a shadow. They don't look back far enough to see who it is they are being chased by. They will not be caught because they run too fast.

PICTURE 9
These two people are lovers who have come out to enjoy the moonlight. They had to go out because the girls father was complaining that it was time the man went. They have gone into the garden and spent so long saying Goodbye that her father has, in disgust, shut and bolted the door on her. She doesn't know this yet, so after the man has gone and she finds that she is locked out she will run after him & ask him to help her to open a window.

PICTURE 10
It is deep into the night and the boy has decided his bedroom is too stuffy. He has opened the window and is looking out at the stars. He is trying to imagine the Universe. He wonders why, out of all the planets and stars that exist, why and how does he come to be living on Earth, one special planet among the billions and trillions there are. He goes back to bed feeling much better and somehow glad. He still thinks about the stars.

Sentence-completion test

1. USUALLY WHEN A GIRL IS WITH HER FATHER he wants her to hold his hand but she hardly ever will.

2. IF SOMEONE IS NOT PART OF THE GROUP they feel sorry for themselves and blame it on the group for leaving them out.

3. OFTEN WHEN THREE PEOPLE ARE TOGETHER two want to go one way and the other wants to go another. These friendships never last.

4. FOR A GIRL PARENTS treat her uniquely if she is the only daughter.

5. WHEN THERE IS NO ONE ELSE AROUND I go up to my bedroom and think about nothing.

6. A GIRL AND A BOY TOGETHER like to be friendly, sometimes very friendly.

7. WHEN SOMEONE GIVES ORDERS TO A GROUP the group waits until everyone decides to obey or disobey. They act as one.

8. IF I AM WITH TWO OTHER PEOPLE I hate being left out of the conversation.

9. OFTEN A GIRL AND HER MOTHER will talk about such silly things and be very great friends.

10. SOMETIMES WHEN I THINK ABOUT MYSELF I wonder what other people think about me.

11. FOR A GIRL BOYS are hardly ever polite but it's different for a woman.

12. IF A PERSON IS ALONE he starts to read—but I never do.

13. WHEN A GIRL IS WITH HER PARENTS she can't talk to her father so well as her mother. Her father might not understand her.

14. NOW AND AGAIN I REALIZE THAT I tend to go along with the gang and not have my own ideas.

Fifteen-year-old girl, the fourth in a family of five, whose father she describes as a 'shitting engineer'.

Picture-story test

PICTURE I
A man with his young son have gone out for the day in the country. They are up high on a hill, when suddenly a thick fog

descends on them. Desperately they tried to find the right pathway down, but without luck. The little boy plonked down on the ground miserably and started to cry, whilst the man was still trying to find the right path. Eventually he gave up, he was standing, trying to see through the fog, when suddenly it seemed thinner, he could see a church steeple. The fog lifted . . .

PICTURE 2

They slowly wandered out of the house, hand in hand, she wanted to cry, but couldn't. He tried to comfort her, and pulled her closer.

Terry and Julie could not marry. Julie had just taken Terry home to meet her parents and hopefully get their consent of marriage, but as soon as her father saw Terry he stormed out, he would see no reason. Terry was coloured. He took Julie's hand and led her to the door, they wandered through the yard, both knowing they could never see each other again, the gate closed behind him, and Julie broke down.

PICTURE 3

The two old ladies sat at each end of the table and Max thought they would NEVER stop reminiscing about the past. He got up to get his cigarettes from the mantelpiece and imediately his old mother started to nag him about 'getting bloody cancer'. Of course the other old hag *will* agree, thought Max; sure enough 'You're right Ethel'.

Max thought he would die if he had to stand this much longer, but what else could he do? A bloke can't live on nothing, just coming out of prison. So he had to live with his nagging mother, who was worse than any bullying warden. Suddenly a letter came through the letter-box. HE'D BEEN EXCEPTED for his job, now he could live alone.

PICTURE 4

'Look at them all', thought Geoff 'all the same, they think it's bloody marvellous, a load of old rubbish is whats in their minds.' The others always stood apart from Geoff, partly because he always seemed to be in another world, and partly because he smelt.

The Institute of Art had taken out a few members of it's classes, to an old ruin that was supposedly 'beautiful', but Geoff was the only one who realy thought it so. He loved old things, he loved anything in connection with the past, his mind would always dream of days gone by, and his eyes always rome to his dry books. The others didn't understand.

PICTURE 5
'Eere whadya fink their doing then?'
'I dunno do I?'
'Sounds a bit rough to me'
'Ere *I* know'
'Bet you don't'
'Bet I do'
'Alright then what is it?'
'Aint tellin' ya'.'
'Aw! Why you swine?'
'Ya *too* young'
'Pooh, *your* only two years older than me.'
'2 years is 2 years'
'Oh c'mon John'
'NO!'
'Quick they're coming out'
'You run that way'
'Alright!'
Pit-pat-pit-pat-pit-pat. They run to the safety of their own bedrooms.

PICTURE 6
My dream was always recurring, sometimes every night, sometimes only once a week. But it terrified me, it awoke in me a fear that I'd never known could exist. I would be standing alone, in an alley, and two men would walk towards me, I'd get a trickle of cold run down my spine, then as they got nearer their faces would turn into a vultures head and their hands into long claws that tore at my hair and ripped my face into shreds, I could feel the pain. Then I awake.

PICTURE 7
'Whats that love?'
'Nothing dad—honest!'

'C'mon what is it?'
'NOTHING'
Nicola fled to the bed and hid the piece of paper under the sheets. Her father just stood in the doorway looking at her, and slowly unfastened his belt. Nicola saw the movement and began to quiver, she screamed, 'Alright dad, alright'.
She snatched the paper from beneath the covers, and gave it to him. It was a note explaining why she had left home. He took her in his arms and begged her not to leave.

PICTURE 8
The crowd shouted and cheered, and laughed and sanged.
For this was the day Ben Hur was hanged. He'd murdered his wife.
He'd battered her in
Oh how the bells chimed
How they did ring.
The rope tightened around his throat pulling his beard like a nany goat's.
His feet swung to and fro
Now the people cried . . .
Oh! they missed him so.
They dressed up in black
And cried night and day.
Now WHO was it that put Ben away?
They hunted him down
They hung him too
Now they're looking for some-one new.

PICTURE 9
'Darling will you marry me?
'No'
'Darling do you love me?
'No'
'You're eyes are like the heavens above. Oh darling you send me in ecstasy.'
'Tut I wonder when this rain'll stop'
'You're red, red lips'
'Probably last till this afternoon'
'Your figure is divine'

'Still you never know could dry up.'
'Darling, I've got a strange feeling you're not listening to me.'
'What's that? Oh yeah! Realy?'
'I've just asked you a very personal question Mavis'
'What? Under a tree in the rain? Not on your life I'll get wet.'
'Oh Mavis'
He storms off in a storm, storming about the storm.

PICTURE 10
I've often tried to wander through thought and space of time.
I wanted to penetrate the deep feeling of my mind. The significance of its being. I tried and tried to look through the windows
of the world. Until one day I heard a fragment of a song 'passing
from dawn to eternity. I want to be, in the warm hold of your
loving mind' then I new, it was Patsy, my lover; the window
opened and I found my way.

Sentence-completion test
1.   USUALLY WHEN A GIRL IS WITH HER FATHER the topic of
conversation is very ordinary and boring.
2.   IF SOMEONE IS NOT PART OF THE GROUP he or she has a
mind of her own and likes to be alone. B.O.
3.   OFTEN WHEN THREE PEOPLE ARE TOGETHER one person
gets left out.
4.   FOR A GIRL PARENTS it is usually quite a nice household to
live in.
5.   WHEN THERE IS NO ONE ELSE AROUND I think a lot.
6.   A GIRL AND A BOY TOGETHER nearly always make love.
7.   WHEN SOMEONE GIVES ORDERS TO A GROUP he is a very
conceited and selfish person.
8.   IF I AM WITH TWO OTHER PEOPLE who are together I hop
out quick.
9.   OFTEN A GIRL AND HER MOTHER can talk infinitely about
girlish problems.
10.   SOMETIMES WHEN I THINK ABOUT MYSELF I wonder what
I'm all about, what other people think of me.
11.   FOR A GIRL BOYS are very necessary and gorgeous hand-
some fantastic, sexy, brilliant, kind, well most of them anyway.
12.   IF A PERSON IS ALONE he or she often does things that they
wouldn't dare do if somebody else were there.

13. WHEN A GIRL IS WITH HER PARENTS she feels ill-at-ease and feels like kicking them.

14. NOW AND AGAIN I REALIZE THAT I should be more considerate towards other people.

Seventeen-year-old girl with one younger brother and one younger sister, whose father she describes as 'officially a rather shady solicitor, but I can't imagine what he does to get the money'.

Picture-story test

PICTURE 1

He is a sad man, alone, he can't get what he wants, or knows he wants, but he can see it or realise it. The light is what he wants. He is an outsider. There is some degree of choice in it, involved at the beginning. He chose to be like this although he had little realisation of the consequences—i.e. most people didnt choose to be like him. There could be another figure in the left corner, crouching or sitting, a woman involved without much realisation in his isolation.

He's right. He's sad. He'll always be alone, and often look at the happy light.

PICTURE 2

Two people, or girl and a boy close together. It is a 'respectable relationship', it is her house and he comes to see her. They dont understand that being sad and poignant in the moonlight is no good if youre on this side of the fence. I wish they were running naked up and down the rather boring mountains and were glad & fierce. They will settle in a comfortable married existence, but not necessarily with each other. Thats immaterial. Parents inside house.

PICTURE 3

Not a poor home. People comfortable, exchanging platitudes after tea or perhaps supper. 'Glow from fireplace lighting up speakers face' Somebody is probably wearing slippers they feel comfortable, they clothes fit them loosely, in the way that they like best, and makes them feel them. The arm on armchair belongs to somebody whose very much at ease. Person standing would be seeing palaces in the fire but I rather doubt. Nothing will happen. They will probably do the same tomorrow.

PICTURE 4
Lots of people in light and shade. The one alone, a boy, could be being a sundial, as he has no-one to talk to, and so is probably thinking important things. The others are a pack of unwilling schoolboys trapped by teacher (dominant head) while he destroys any interest they might have had in the area.
The boys are the fools who didnt escape. The single boy doesnt notice them and is a much nicer presence. The group are being indoctrinated. But half willingly. The other will be O.K. The group will be middle class slobs.

PICTURE 5
The small boy has just been very polite to somebody who he didnt know who opened the door. He asked to see someone, another child, and the mother has gone to fetch him. The little boy is not a tease. The bigger person has told the little boy to do this, and soon the little boy will twist towards him anxiously to know if he has to go on and is it the right thing.

PICTURE 6
Here, there is a large pit in the foreground, into which somebody has just fallen. Three people are standing around rather aimlessly, wondering if she's alright. None of them are very perturbed because there was a large flood recently which drained away leaving huge holes which people fall down a lot. The light between them is a fuzz car which is blaring away tearing out their ears, but they are so depressed and insensitive that they dont even move. They are not interesting. The person in the pit is happy.

PICTURE 7
Some poor kid who was having fun has just woked up to see that the person who 'will come and get you if you dont go to bed on time' has come. The child is very frightened, is trying to creep away. The person is not female but not necessarily male and has not spoken but just loomed. There is a great raging fire

downstairs and the staircase is burnt away. The little boy will be carried away down through the flames.

PICTURE 8
Beggars, poor people, peasants, mutilated idiots, all standing at the bottom of the steps of the enormous palace which their lord has built with the taxes he extorts from them. They are frightened of him, it is very cold and they are asking for a day off. However its a rather feudal set up and he is menacing & they believe it is their duty to honour him etc. The only one who feels some indignation is the one to the right with arms raised in impotent anger as they are sent away without a day off.

PICTURE 9
Theyre standing under a tree, a boy and girl after having just escaped from the horrible house and they were going to run away for ever and ever but she has forgotten her pills and they cant decide whether it would be worth risking it to go back. In the end they'll not go back for the pills, and decide to try without and she'll get pregnant and they wont have an ideal situation and she from such a rich upbringing will be forced to scrub floors to give herself a miscarriage.

PICTURE 10
He's nearly out but he's just looked back and its going to be fatal. He is just a person who thought he'd like to be alone, for a while and he might have made it. Inside there is a scene of debauchery with wine flowing and people fucking behind sofa's as they are still prudish. He's glad but sad. He wants to go but he regrets leaving all this as there's some chick hanging around he'll be okay in a boring way, which is worst of all.

Sentence-completion test
1. USUALLY WHEN A GIRL IS WITH HER FATHER she is disagreeing with what he is saying.
2. IF SOMEONE IS NOT PART OF THE GROUP they probably make up better fairy tales without bitchery.
3. OFTEN WHEN THREE PEOPLE ARE TOGETHER they laugh a lot and I like the other two.

4.   FOR A GIRL PARENTS are a drag.

5.   WHEN THERE IS NO ONE ELSE AROUND I am happy.

6.   A GIRL AND BOY TOGETHER should be careful because when you get an abortion on NHS its usually a hysterectomy.

7.   WHEN SOMEBODY GIVES ORDERS TO A GROUP the group should not obey automatically but should consider what is right.

8.   IF I AM WITH TWO OTHER PEOPLE and they are nice I like them.

9.   OFTEN A GIRL AND HER MOTHER are estranged in her adolescence quite often theyre not.

10.   SOMETIMES WHEN I THINK ABOUT MYSELF I feel depressed.

11.   FOR A GIRL BOYS are exciting or boring, but still people. I wish I went to school with them, for then some people wouldnt be as perverted as they are.

12.   IF A PERSON IS ALONE they will be sad if its not by choice.

13.   WHEN A GIRL IS WITH HER PARENTS they can be mutually embarassed or quite enjoy each others company.

14.   NOW AND AGAIN I REALIZE THAT I talk too much.

Eighteen-year-old girl who has one older sister, and whose father is an office manager for a branch of a world-wide firm.

Picture-story test

PICTURE I

The people seem to be symbolic. The central figure, the man, seems strong—the leader, whilst the other two figures listen and seem submissive. The figure on the left is of a woman hugging her knees, almost as if she is listening to a story. The figure on the left seems melancholy, almost lethargic. She seems to be intent upon her own thoughts, perhaps listening inattentively though. The 'story' does not seem to be going to 'turn out' at all. The picture evokes mood and one feels that this situation would continue for some time without changing at all—the man remaining dominant and the woman submissive.

PICTURE 2

The way the people look at the scenery suggests that they are in a place they have never been before. The boy and girl seem in love and are gazing in awe at the scenery. They stand looking, but one does not feel that they are particularly intense. One supposes that they will draw near each other and kiss. The conclusion is obvious from the picture which evokes no deep feelings and seems rather too hackneyed.

PICTURE 3
There is an air of pending disaster in the picture. The two figures seated seem exceedingly comfortable and are obviously not young. The man standing, younger than the other two people, leans, and seems on the point of telling the people, his parents, probably, something very important. He seems to be working to sum up all his courage to utter the words, and when he finds them the father will say nothing, just look, and the mother will cry and be very sad. The son will become angry as a defence against the hurt he has caused his parents, breaking up the warm, peaceful atmosphere of the house.

PICTURE 4
The Outsider—the Outcast. The one the others won't associate with. He stands alone wanting to be accepted into the group and yet not daring to say anything. He has been rejected by them, he has no friends. They are safe in their little group: the selfish people. They do not think what it would be like if the positions were reversed. They chatter, whisper, giggle, tell jokes, and look towards him—never feeling qualms of guilt. And so they will stand for some long time, the watcher and the watched until the group move off to have some fun and only the watcher is left.

PICTURE 5
The boy waiting outside, waiting to be disciplined. He must retain his military bearing. He must not break down and cry even though he is only a little boy and worried out of his mind. He must not even show the guard who has brought him to his superiors what he feels. The guard stands, impassive. Did this same situation ever happen to him. He recovered. Perhaps when older the boy will be just as impassive and it will be his turn to take small boys to his superiors, they quaking whilst he stands upright. And suddenly the door opens wider—he must go in— 'into the valley of death . . . '

PICTURE 6
Across the river they shout. They can't cross. It is forbidden—
penalty death? ! ! They are so near and yet so far. They can
make themselves understood to each other, but with difficulty.
The frustration of not being able to see each other properly, not
being able to touch each other. At least there are two on the right
bank; they can console each other when the three must take
leave of each other. But the one, the lone one. He must go back,
lonely, depressed. Walk away, a single spot into the distance,
back to what? a void, an emptiness, a nothingness. And the
situation won't change; it will be so for many many years to
come—the barrier ! !

PICTURE 7
The naughty child scrambles back into bed. The sight of her
father is enough to provoke immediate obedience to past com-
mands. What had she fetched? Was she looking in the mirror,
trying on her mother's clothes, her sister's make-up? Was she
'putting her hair up?' She was trying to be grown up. And so
when her father comes, she is torn from her dream world of
adults back to the world of children who are only dominated
by adults. And all the time, her father stands in the doorway, a
symbol of strength, without physical action he forces her to do
his bidding merely by his presence—the power of the 'grown-up'.

PICTURE 8
The fright—the terror—the complete horror. The person comes,
he advances, unrelentlessly. The crowd start to panic, they
realise what will happen, something terrible will happen to them.
The wrath of the man will fall upon them. A head turns here, a
hand is raised in defence, somebody half turns to flee, and
people cower together—the immediate reaction, which is so
useless. The figure advances menacingly, on, and on, and on,
and on; the crowd's fever mounts to a pitch; they can't move
back and on the figure comes: he's nearly upon them, he is
suffocating them—and on and on and on he comes,—on and
on and on . . .

PICTURE 9
They shelter, for no obvious reason. There is no rain, no hail

no lightening. The house is not falling down. They just stand. The two people stand and stare, look at something not very interesting. They wile away the time and another half hour is lost. They lean against the tree lazily, but there is no real feeling of sultriness or anything suggesting why they should do so. They do nothing and are nothing and will move away from the tree, and walk, continuing to do, and say nothing—their lives are a nothing!

PICTURE 10
What can he see—this romantic. He imagines what is up there in the sky. How could those pieces of glass, glittering glass have such perfect shapes? How could they exist in that stretch of colour? They are like holes pierced in a sheet of paper? They had been sprinkled. He imagines himself jumping from star to star through the window—a mixture of Peter Pan, another the Sylph de la Rose. With such intensity can man live? How can man be content with the ordinary things of life? Man wants to grasp that mystery, to keep it to have it, to understand it's unfathomable beauty.

Sentence-completion test
1.   USUALLY WHEN A GIRL IS WITH HER FATHER she takes his arm.
2.   IF SOMEONE IS NOT PART OF THE GROUP they are isolated and so lonely.
3.   OFTEN WHEN THREE PEOPLE ARE TOGETHER two dislike the third.
4.   FOR A GIRL PARENTS must be understanding.
5.   WHEN THERE IS NO ONE ELSE AROUND I sit and dream of everything and nothing.
6.   A GIRL AND A BOY TOGETHER often are completely different from how they are with other friends.
7.   WHEN SOMEONE GIVES ORDERS TO A GROUP they don't always obey.
8.   IF I AM WITH TWO OTHER PEOPLE I hope I like at least one of them.
9.   OFTEN A GIRL AND HER MOTHER don't 'get on'.
10.   SOMETIMES WHEN I THINK ABOUT MYSELF I wonder just what I am.

11.   FOR A GIRL BOYS can be something extraordinary or the cause of most sadness.

12.   IF A PERSON IS ALONE he obviously is either lonely or alone from choice.

13.   WHEN A GIRL IS WITH HER PARENTS she feels very proud.

14.   NOW AND AGAIN I REALIZE THAT I should remember that I'm not perfect so why should other people be.

Bibliography

ACKERMAN, N. W. (1958) *The Psychodynamics of Family*, Basic Books, New York.

ACKERMAN, N. W. (1962) 'Adolescent problems: a symptom of family disorder', *Family Process*, 1, 202–13.

ADELSON, J., GREEN, B. and O'NEILL, R. P. (1969) 'The growth of the idea of law in adolescence', *Developmental Psychology*, 1(4), 327–32.

ADELSON, J. and O'NEILL, R. P. (1966) 'The growth of political ideas in adolescence', *Journal of Personality and Social Psychology*, 4, 295–306.

ALDOUS, J. and HILL, R. (1965) 'Social cohesion, lineage type, and intergenerational transmission', *Social Forces*, 43, 471–82.

BANDURA, A. (1972) 'The stormy decade: fact or fiction', in *Issues in Adolescent Psychology* (2nd edn) ed. D. Rogers, Appleton-Century-Crofts, New York.

BANDURA, A. and WALTERS, R. H. (1959) *Adolescent Aggression*, Ronald, New York.

BEALER, R. C., WILLITS, F. and MAIDA, P. R. (1969) 'The rebellious youth sub-culture—a myth', in *Issues in Adolescent Psychology*, 1st edn, ed. D. Rogers, Appleton-Century-Crofts, New York.

BELL, R. R. (1966) *Pre-marital Sex in a Changing Society*, Prentice-Hall, Englewood Cliffs, New Jersey.

BENGTSON, V. L. (1970) 'The generation gap', *Youth and Society*, 2(1), 7–32.

BLOS, P. (1962) *On Adolescence*, Collier-Macmillan, London.

BLOS, P. (1965) 'The initial stage of male adolescence', *Psychoanalytic Study of the Child*, 20, 145–64.

BLOS, P. (1967) 'The second individuation process of adolescence', *Psychoanalytic Study of the Child*, 22, 162–86.

BOLTON, C. D. and KAMMEYER, K. C. (1967) *The University Student: A Study of Student Behaviour and Values*, University Press, New Haven, Connecticut.

BOWERMAN, C. E. and KINCH, J. W. (1959) 'Changes in family and peer orientation of children between the fourth and tenth grades', *Social Forces*, 37, 206–11.

BOWLBY, J. (1969) *Attachment and loss*, vol. I, Hogarth Press, London.

BRIM, O. G. (1965) 'Adolescent personality as self-other systems', *Journal of Marriage and the Family*, 27, 156–62.

BRONFENBRENNER, U. and RICCIUTI, H. N. (1960) 'The appraisal of personality characteristics in children', in *Handbook of Research Methods in Child Development*, ed. P. Mussen, John Wiley, London.

BURCHINAL, L. G. (1964) 'Adolescent dating attitudes and behaviour', in *Handbook of Marriage and the Family*, ed. A. T. Christensen, Rand McNally, Chicago.

BUROS, O. K. (1965) *The Sixth Mental Measurement Yearbook*, Gryphon Press, Highland Park, New Jersey.

CARLSON, R. (1965) 'Stability and change in the adolescent's self-image', *Child Development*, 36, 659–66.

COLEMAN, J. C. (1967) 'Stimulus factors in the relation between fantasy and behaviour', *Journal of Projective Techniques and Personality Assessment*, 31, 68–74.

COLEMAN, J. C. (1968) 'Rorschach content as a means of studying child development', *Journal of Projective Techniques and Personality Assessment*, 32, 435–42.

COLEMAN, J. C. (1969a) 'The levels hypothesis: a reexamination and reorientation', *Journal of Projective Techniques and Personality Assessment*, 33, 118–22.

COLEMAN, J. C. (1969b) 'Changes in T.A.T. responses as a function of age', *Journal of Genetic Psychology*, 114, 171–8.

COLEMAN, J. C. (1969c) 'The perception of interpersonal relationships during adolescence', *British Journal of Educational Psychology*, 39, 253–60.

COLEMAN, J. C. (1970) 'The study of adolescent development using a sentence-completion method', *British Journal of Educational Psychology*, 40, 27–34.

COLEMAN, J. S. (1961) *The Adolescent Society*, Free Press, New York.

COSTANZA, P. and SHAW, M. (1966) 'Conformity as a function of age level', *Child Development*, 37, 967–75.

DEUTSCH, H. (1944) *Psychology of Women*, vol. I, Grune & Stratton, New York.

DOUVAN, E. and ADELSON, J. (1966) *The Adolescent Experience*, John Wiley, New York.

DOUVAN, E. and GOLD, H. (1966) 'Modal patterns in American adolescence', in *Review of Child Development Research*, vol. 2, ed. L. Hoffman, and M. Hoffman, Russell Sage Foundation, New York.

DUNPHY, D. C. (1963) 'The social structure of urban adolescent peer groups', *Sociometry*, 26, 230–46.

ELDER, G. H. (1968) 'Adolescent socialization and development', in *Handbook of Personality Theory and Research*, ed. E. Borgatta and W. Lambert, Rand McNally, Chicago.

ELKIND, D. (1967) 'Egocentrism in adolescence', *Child Development*, 38, 1025–34.

ENGEL, M. (1959) 'The stability of the self-concept in adolescence', *Journal of Abnormal and Social Psychology*, 58, 211–15.

EPPEL, M. and EPPEL, E. (1962) 'The views of some adults on the standards and behaviour of adolescents', *British Journal of Sociology*, 13(3), 32.

ERIKSON, E. H. (1963) *Childhood and Society*, Norton, New York.

ERIKSON, E. H. (1968) *Identity: Youth and Crisis*, Faber & Faber, London.

ERIKSON, E. H. (1969) 'The problem of ego identity', in *Adolescent Development: Readings in Research and Theory*, ed. M. Gold and E. Douvan, Allyn & Bacon, Boston, Mass.

FAIRBAIRN, W. R. (1952) *Psycho-analytic Studies of Personality*, Tavistock, London.

FRANK, L. (1939) 'Projective methods for the study of personality', *Journal of Psychology*, 8, 389–413.

FREUD, A. (1937) *The Ego and the Mechanisms of Defence*, Hogarth Press, London.

GOLD, M. and DOUVAN, E. (eds.) (1966) *Adolescent Development: Readings in Research and Theory*, Allyn & Bacon, Boston, Mass.

GOLDBERG, L. R. and WERTS, C. E. (1966) 'The reliability of clinician's judgement', *Journal of Consulting Psychology*, 30, 199–206.

GREENACRE, P. (1970) 'Youth, growth and violence', *Psychoanalytic Study of the Child*, 25, 340–59.

HALL, G. S. (1904) *Adolescence: Its Psychology and Its Relations to Physiology, Anthropology, Sociology, Sex, Crime, Religion and Education*, vols 1 and 2, D. Appleton, New York.

HARVEY, O. J. and RUTHERFORD, J. (1960) 'Status in the informal group: influence and influencibility at differing age levels', *Child Development*, 31, 377–85.

HENRY, W. E. (1960) 'Projective techniques', in *Handbook of Research Methods in Child Development*, ed. P. Mussen, John Wiley, London.

HESS, R. D. and GOLDBLATT, I. (1957) 'The status of adolescents in American society: a problem in social identity', *Child Development*, 28, 459–68.

HILL, R. and ALDOUS, J. (1969) 'Socialization for marriage and parenthood', in *Handbook of Socialization Theory and Research*, ed. D. Goslin, Rand McNally, Chicago.

HORROCKS, J. E. and BAKER, M. (1951) 'A study of the friendship fluctuations of preadolescents', *Journal of Genetic Psychology*, 78, 131–44.

HORROCKS, J. E. and THOMPSON, G. G. (1946) 'A study of friendship fluctuations of rural boys and girls', *Journal of Genetic Psychology*, 69, 189–98.

HORROCKS, J. and WEINBERG, S. (1970) 'Psychological needs and their development during adolescence', *Journal of Psychology*, 74, 51–69.

HUTT, C. (1972) *Males and Females*, Penguin, Harmondsworth.

KAGAN, J. and MOSS, H. (1962) *From Birth to Maturity*, John Wiley, New York.

KATZ, P. and ZIGLER, E. (1967) 'Self-image disparity: a developmental approach', *Journal of Personality and Social Psychology*, 5, 186–95.

KENISTON, K. (1968) *Young Radicals*, Harcourt, Brace & World, New York.

LANDSBAUM, J. and WILLIS, R. (1971) 'Conformity in early and late adolescence', *Developmental Psychology*, 4, 334–7.

LICCIONE, J. V. (1955) 'The changing family relationships of adolescent girls', *Journal of Abnormal and Social Psychology*, 51, 521–6.

MAHLER, M. S. (1963) 'Thoughts about development and individuation', *Psychoanalytic Study of the Child*, 18, 307–24.

MANNHEIM, K. (1943) *Diagnosis of Our Time*, Routledge & Kegan Paul, London.

MURRAY, H. A. (1943) *Thematic Apperception Test Manual*, Harvard University Press, Cambridge, Mass.

MUSGROVE, F. (1964) *Youth and the Social Order*, Routledge & Kegan Paul, London.

MUSSEN, P. (ed.) (1960) *Handbook of Research in Child Development*, John Wiley, London.

MUUSS, R. E. (1962) *Theories of Adolescence*, Random House, New York.

NEWMAN, F. M. (1966) 'Adolescent's constructs of authority figures: a methodological study', *Journal of General Psychology*, 74, 319–38.

OFFER, D. (1969) *The Psychological World of the Teen-ager*, Basic Books, New York.

OFFER, D., MARCUS, D. and OFFER, J. (1970) 'A longitudinal study of normal adolescent boys', *American Journal of Psychiatry*, 126, 917–24.

PHILLIPSON, H. (1955) *The Object Relations Technique*, Tavistock, London.

POWELL, M. (1955) 'Age and sex differences in degree of conflict within certain areas of psychological adjustment', *Psychological Monographs*, 69, (no. 387).

REISS, I. R. (1968) 'America's sex standards—how and why they're changing', *Trans-action*, 5(4), 26–32.

ROGERS, D. (1972) 'Stage theory and critical period as related to adolescence', in *Issues in Adolescent Psychology*, 2nd edn, ed. D. Rogers, Appleton-Century-Crofts, New York.

ROOT, N. (1957) 'A neurosis in adolescence', *Psychoanalytic Study of the Child*, 12, 320–34.

ROSENBERG, M. (1965) *Society and the Adolescent Self-Image*, Princeton University Press, Princeton, New Jersey.

SARBIN, T. R. (1964) 'Role theoretical interpretation of psychological change', in *Personality Change*, ed. P. Worchel and D. Byrne, John Wiley, New York.

SCHAFFER, H. R. (1971) *The Growth of Sociability*, Penguin, Harmondsworth.

SCHOFIELD, M. (1965) *The Sexual Behaviour of Young People*, Longmans Green, London.

SPIEGEL, L. A. (1951) 'A review of contributions to a psychoanalytic theory of adolescence', *Psychoanalytic Study of the Child*, 6, 375–93.

SPIEGEL, L. A. (1961) 'Disorder and consolidation in adolescence', *Journal of the American Psychoanalytic Association*, 9, 406–17.

STIERLIN, H. and RAVENSCROFT, K. (1972) 'Varieties of adolescent "separation conflicts" ', *British Journal of Medical Psychology*, 45, 299–313.

SULLIVAN, H. S. (1950) 'Illusion of personal individuality', *Psychiatry*, 13, 317–32.

SULLIVAN, H. S. (1953) *The Interpersonal Theory of Psychiatry*, Norton, New York.

TANNER, J. M. (1962) *Growth at Adolescence*, Blackwell, Oxford.

THOMAS, L. E. (1971) 'Family correlates of student political activism', *Developmental Psychology*, 4(2), 206–14.

THOMPSON, C. M. (1964) 'H. S. Sullivan', in *Interpersonal Psychoanalysis: Selected papers of Clara M. Thompson*, ed. M. R. Green, Basic Books, New York.

THOMPSON, G. G. and HORROCKS, J. E. (1947) 'A study of the friendship fluctuations of urban boys and girls', *Journal of Genetic Psychology*, 70, 53–63.

WALSH, R. (1970) 'Intergenerational transmission of sexual standards', quoted in Bengtson, V. L. (1970), 'The generation gap', *Youth and Society*, 2(1), 7–32.

WEINER, I. B. (1970) *Psychological Disturbance in Adolescence*, John Wiley, New York.

WESTBY, D. and BRAUNGART, R. (1968) 'Utopian mentality and conservatism. The case of the Young Americans for Freedom', quoted in Bengtson, V. L. (1970), 'The generation gap', *Youth and Society*, 2(1), 7–32.

WILLMOTT, P. (1966) *Adolescent Boys of East London*, Routledge & Kegan Paul, London.

WYATT, F. (1967) 'How objective is objectivity?', *Journal of Projective Techniques and Personality Assessment*, 31, 3–19.

YARROW, L. J. (1964) 'Separation from parents during early childhood', in *Review of Child Development Research*, vol. 1, ed. M. Hoffman and L. Hoffman, Russell Sage Foundation, New York.

Index

Erikson, E. H., 2, 3, 24, 39, 42ff, 144

Fairbairn, W. R., 31
Father: attitudes to, 73, 78, 80; occupation of, 28
Fear: in group situation, 128ff, 143; of solitude, 35–8, 139
'Feel Different', 80ff, 139, 141
Fixation, 2
Formal operations, 5
Frank, L. 29
Freud, A., 12
Freud, S., 12, 151
Friendship, stability of, 90–2; *see also* Peers
Frustration, 80ff, 141

Generation gap, 16, 17, 69
Gold, M., 15, 69, 91
Goldberg, L. R., 30
Goldblatt, I., 74
Green, B., 124, 125
Greenacre, P., 13
Growth, 26, 27

Hall, G. S., 12, 13
Harvey, O. J., 109, 115
Henry, W. E., 29
Hess, R. D., 74
Hill, R., 17
Homosexuality, 66, 67
Horrocks, J. E., 90, 123
Hutt, C., 143

Identification, 115ff
Identity, 3, 14, 38–40, 42ff, 138, 139, 144; crisis, 39, 42ff; diffusion, 3, 14, 39; present and future, 47, 52, 138, 139
'Imaginary audience', 5, 6
Impulse control, 38, 61, 134, 138, 139
Independence, 15, 16, 68ff, 110ff, 139ff
Intelligence, 28
Interview, 18, 28ff, 71

Kagan, J., 38, 83, 143
Kammeyer, K. C., 123
Katz, P., 41
Keniston, K., 123
Kinch, J. W., 74
Kissing, 55ff

Landsbaum, J., 110
Laws, adolescent's concept of, 124, 125
Levels of personality, 18
Liccione, J. V., 72
Longitudinal method, 26, 155

Mahler, M. S., 8
Maida, P. R., 15
Mannheim, K., 19
Marcus, D., 15
MMPI, 40
Moss, H., 38, 83, 143
Mother, attitudes to, 73, 78, 80
Murray, H. A., 31, 162
Musgrove, F., 29, 73
Mussen, P., 26
Muuss, R. E., x

Object constancy (object permanence), 4, 7, 34
Object relations theory, 31
Offer, D., 15, 69
O'Neill, R. P., 123, 124, 125, 134
Orientation: to parents, 74; personal-social, 41
ORT, 31, 160–2

Peers, 90ff, 107ff, 142ff
'Personal fable', 6
Phillipson, H., 31, 160
Piaget, J., 1, 2, 151
Politics: activism in, 17, 123, *see also* Revolutionary behaviour; adolescent's ideas of, 123ff
Popularity, 56, 110
Powell, M., 29, 55, 56, 57, 71, 72, 93
Power, of the group, 107, 109ff, 118ff
Pre-operational thought, 4
Projective test, 18, 28ff